# GREEN LINE NEW 4

## Bayern

Lösungsheft zum
Trainingsbuch
Schulaufgaben

LEARNING ENGLISH

Klett

LEARNING ENGLISH **GREEN LINE NEW 4**
Ausgabe für Bayern

# Lösungsheft zum Trainingsbuch Schulaufgaben

**von**
Robert Bauer, Nürnberg; Peter Müller, Herzogenaurach; Mechthild Murau, Burgthann

**sowie**
Faith Puleston, Wetter; Jennifer Wood B. A., Bristol

**Illustrationen**
Dorothee Wolters, Köln

**Zeichenerklärung**
⨀1 Übungen mit diesem Symbol verweisen auf die hinten im Trainingsbuch eingeklebte CD. Die Ziffer kennzeichnet die Tracknummer. Die Hörtexte sind nicht abgedruckt.

**Bild- und Textquellenverzeichnis**
COV: (1) Avenue Images GmbH/Corbis RF; (2) iStockphoto/RF/Travis; (3) Corbis/Zaunders; (4) Avenue Images GmbH/Rubberball RF; S. 3: Bananastock RF; S. 6: Fotosearch RF/Brand X Pictures; S. 7: MEV; S. 8: (1–2) Klett-Archiv/Negenborn; Text S. 10: Safe Outback Travel, J. Absalom, The Five Mile Press Pty Ltd.; S. 11: Corel Corporation; S. 12: MEV; Text S. 12: www.planetozkids.com; S. 13: Corbis/GRAY/Reuters; S. 14: Picture-Alliance/dpa; S. 15: Wikimedia Foundation Inc./Public Domain; S. 16: (1, 9) Corbis/Bettmann; (2) Klett-Archiv; (4–5, 7) AKG; (6) Gutenberg-Museum; (8) Corbis/Hellier; Text S. 20–21: Discovering Dartmoor, Devon; S. 20: Alamy Images RF/thislife pictures RF; S. 21: iStockphoto/RF/Clark; S. 24: The Heritage Foundation, Washington DC; Text S. 27: Devon Explore, Devon; S. 28: (1) Avenue Images GmbH/Corbis RF; (2) Corbis/LWA-Welstead; (3) Fotosearch RF/PhotoDisc; S. 36: (1–2, 5, 7, 9) MEV, Augsburg; (4) Höllerer; (6) Lade/Röhrig; (8) Avenue Images GmbH/Corbis RF; (10) Creativ Collection Verlag GmbH; S. 39: Wikimedia Foundation Inc./Public Domain; S. 40: (1) Fotofinder/Freelens/Tack; (2–3): Mauritius/age; Text S. 40: Plimoth Plantation; S. 41: (1) Ingram Publishing; (2) MEV; S. 45: Klett-Archiv; S. 48: Mauritius; S. 50: (1) Mauritius/age; (2) Ingram Publishing; S. 58: Bananastock RF; S. 59: Klett-Archiv/Schiffels; Text S. 62: Australian Government, Belconnen; S. 63: Fotosearch RF; S. 64: (1) Fotosearch RF/Image 100; (2–3) Getty Images/Eyewire

**Copyrightangaben zur CD**
**Aufnahmeleitung:** Ernst Klett Verlag
**Regie:** Andrew Branch für RBA Productions
**Sprecherinnen und Sprecher:** Tim Bentinck, Nick Boulton, Brian Bowles, Andrew Branch, Jenny Bryce, Elaine Claxton, Jane Collingwood, Emma D'Inverno, DeNica Fairman, Rupert Farley, Teresa Gallagher, James Goode, Nigel Greaves, Jo Hall, John Hasler, Sam Peter Jackson, Kate Lock, Allan Marriott, Simon Mattacks, Nicolette McKenzie, Kris Milnes, Juliet Prague, Steven Webb, Jane Whittenshaw, Daniel Wilson, David Wilson, Jo Wyatt
**Tontechnik:** Dave Harris at Air-Edel Studios, London;
**Schnitt und Mischung:** Mark Smith und Air-Edel Studios, London
**Presswerk:** P+O Compact-Disc GmbH, Diepholz.

1. Auflage
Alle Drucke dieser Auflage sind unverändert und können im Unterricht nebeneinander verwendet werden. Die letzten Zahlen bezeichnen jeweils die Auflage und das Jahr des Druckes.
Das Werk und seine Teile sind urheberrechtlich geschützt. Jede Nutzung in anderen als den gesetzlich zugelassenen Fällen bedarf der vorherigen schriftlichen Einwilligung des Verlags. Hinweis zu § 52 a UrhG: Weder das Werk noch seine Teile dürfen ohne eine solche Einwilligung eingescannt und in ein Netzwerk eingestellt werden.

**Redaktion:** Gaby Bauer-Negenborn (Außenredaktion)
**Herstellung:** Marietta Heymann

Umschlaggestaltung: Christian Dekelver, Weinstadt
Reproduktion: Meyle + Müller, Medienmanagement, Pforzheim
Druck: Medien Druck Unterland GmbH, Flein
Printed in Germany
ISBN-13: 978-3-12-547273-0
ISBN-10: 3-12-547273-3

1 $^{5\ 4\ 3\ 2\ 1}$ | 2010 09 08 07 06

Dies gilt auch für Intranets von Schulen und sonstigen Bildungseinrichtungen.

Fotomechanische oder andere Wiedergabeverfahren nur mit Genehmigung des Verlags.

© Ernst Klett Verlag GmbH, Stuttgart 2006
Internetadresse: www.klett.de
Alle Rechte vorbehalten

# Unit 1 intro: Down under

## 1 Vocabulary: Australian wildlife

**Across →**
1. Animals with eight legs.
2. It is not really a bear.
3. A really cute animal.
4. Many Australian snakes are very …
5. These birds can't fly.
6. This animal can jump.
7. In some parts of Australia, you should not go swimming in rivers, as they are full of …
8. Bites from some of the (see 1.) that live in Australia can be …
9. … are fish with very sharp teeth.

**Down ↓**
10. Nickname[1] for Australia.

Crossword answers:
1 SPIDERS
2 KOALA
3 WOMBAT
4 POISONOUS
5 EMUS
6 KANGAROO
7 CROCODILES
8 DEADLY
9 SHARKS

[1] ['nɪkneɪm] – Spitzname

## 2 Mixed bag: Error-spotting

There are two mistakes in each line of the following text. Underline them and write down the correct words on the right.

Australia is the <u>dryest</u> continent. In most <u>part's</u> of the outback, — *driest, parts*
<u>their</u> is very little rain. This is one reason <u>because</u> most people — *there, why*
<u>living</u> on or near the coast. There are huge <u>cow</u> stations in — *live, cattle*
the outback, and Australia has more <u>sheeps</u> <u>then</u> people, too. — *sheep, than*
Sydney is the <u>bigest</u> city in the country with about four <u>millions</u> — *biggest, million*
<u>inhabitents</u>. <u>It's</u> most famous landmarks are the Opera House — *inhabitants, Its*
and the Harbour <u>bridge</u>, and Bondi Beach is Sydney's <u>popularest</u> — *Bridge, most popular*
beach. Sydneysiders[1] are <u>realy</u> keen <u>of</u> swimming and other — *really, (keen) on*
water sports, so in <u>Summer</u> there are always a <u>lots</u> of people on — *summer, a lot/lots*
the city's many <u>wonderfull</u> <u>beachs</u>. — *wonderful, beaches*

[1] ['sɪdnɪˌsaɪdəz] – people who live in Sydney

---

# Unit 1 language A: New neighbours

## 1 Writing: What did Matt say?

a) Matt told and asked Lin a lot of things.

1. "Where did you live before you moved to Sydney?"
2. "My parents bought our house when I was a baby."
3. "You should come over to our place tomorrow."
4. "How long has your family been living in Australia?"
5. "In summer we often have barbecues in our garden."
6. "I hope you'll go to my school."
7. "There are a lot of nice people in my class."
8. "Have you met my parents?"

b) The next day Lin told her family what Matt had said or asked. Use the following verbs:

want to know (2x)   ask   mention   tell   point out   say (2x)

1. Lin: Matt *wanted to know where we/I had lived before we moved to Sydney.*
2. He *pointed out that his parents had bought their house when he was a baby.*
3. He *said I should come/go over to their place today.*
4. He *wanted to know how long my/our family had been living in Australia.*
5. He *mentioned that in summer they often had barbecues in their garden.*
6. He *told me that he hoped I would go to his school.*
7. He *said there were a lot of nice people in his class.*
8. He *asked me if I had met his parents.*

## 2 C-test: Asians in Australia    Complete the missing words.

The Wangs are new in Rockdale, a s*uburb* of Sydney. Like the Wangs, a lot of Sydney's four million i*nhabitants* were born in Asia. They came to Australia as i*mmigrants* from China, Malaysia, Thailand, Indonesia and other P*acific* Rim countries. Most of these people didn't *waste* time after they had a*rrived* in Australia, but started to *work* hard immediately. They didn't d*oubt* that they could 'make it' there, they b*elieved* in their own success. Of course, Australia is a very important t*rading* partner for most Asian countries, so many Asians who come to Australia work for c*ompanies* from their home countries.

---

# Unit 1 language A

## 3 Grammar: What Lin would like Matt to do

When the Wangs were saying goodbye to the Donovans, Lin said many things to Matt. Use indirect commands and the following verbs to report what she said.

tell   advise   want   invite   ask   warn

1. "You can come and visit me any time."
   *Lin invited Matt to come/go and visit her any time.*

2. "It's best to knock at our door, as the door bell doesn't work."
   *She advised him to knock at their door, as the door bell didn't/doesn't work.*

3. "But stay away from Lizzy, our cat."
   *Lin warned Matt to stay away from Lizzy, their cat.*

4. "It would be great if you brought some of your favourite CDs."
   *She wanted him to bring/take some of his favourite CDs.*

5. "Could you let me have a look at the books you use at school?"
   *Lin asked Matt to let her have a look at the books he used at school.*

6. "Please don't come over before 10 o'clock on Sundays."
   *She told him not to come/go over before 10 o'clock on Sundays.*

## 4 Speaking: Ms Beumer

After school Lin reported a conversation with her teacher to her mother.

> Today I was asked by my Maths teacher, Ms Beumer if I had learned to speak English in China. So I told her I hadn't, as I'd never been to China! She said she was sorry, and explained to me that she had an Asian student in another class who'd only been living in Australia for a year, but already spoke perfect English. I told her that we'd only just moved to Sydney, so that's why I was new there. Then she told me not to worry, as that was a good school, and asked me if there was anything she could do for me. But I said I was fine and added that I'd come back to her when I needed help.

Now write down Lin's conversation with her teacher. Add words to make it sound better where necessary.

Ms Beumer: *Did you learn to speak English in China?*

Lin: *No, I didn't. I've never been to China.*

Ms Beumer: *Oh, I'm sorry. You see, I have an Asian student in another class who has only been living in Australia for a year,*

*but he already speaks perfect English.*

Lin: *We've only just moved to Sydney, so that's why I'm new here.*

Ms Beumer: *Well, don't worry, this is a good school.*

*Is there anything I can do for you?*

Lin: *No, thanks. I'm fine. I'll come back to you when I need help.*

---

## 5 Mediation: Can you tell me the way to …, please?

One day Matt's classmate Rob met a German tourist in downtown Sydney. As Rob's parents are from Nuremberg[1], Rob speaks German.

*Tourist:* Entschuldigung, sprichst du Deutsch?
*Rob:* Ja, das tue ich, Sie haben Glück.
*Tourist:* Wohnst du hier?
*Rob:* Naja, ich wohne nicht im Stadtzentrum, sondern in einem Vorort.
*Tourist:* Aber du weißt, wie man zum Opernhaus kommt, oder?
*Rob:* Na klar, weiß ich das.
*Tourist:* Bitte sag es mir!
*Rob:* Gehen Sie diese Straße entlang, bis Sie zu einem Souvenirgeschäft kommen. Biegen Sie dort nach rechts ab und wenden Sie sich an der nächsten Straße nach links. Nach etwa 100 Metern sehen Sie das Opernhaus.
*Tourist:* Vielen Dank. Warum sprichst du so gut Deutsch?
*Rob:* Meine Eltern kamen vor 20 Jahren als Einwanderer aus Deutschland hierher.
*Tourist:* Sag Ihnen, dass du einen Rainer aus Schweinfurt getroffen hast.
*Rob:* Das mache ich. Wiedersehen.

[1] ['njʊərəmbɜːg] – Nürnberg

Later Rob reported this conversation to Matt. Use the following verbs:

explain   say   ask   want to know   tell   answer   advise

Rob: Today I met a tourist in George Street. I don't know why, but he asked me if I spoke German. Do I look German? Well, I said *I did* and *told* him he *was lucky*. So he *asked me if I lived here/there.* *I said I didn't live in the city centre,* but in a suburb. He asked me *if I knew how to get to the Opera* House. *I answered that of course I did, so he* asked me to tell him. *I advised him to go down that street until he got to a* souvenir shop. I *told him to turn right there and left at the next street.* *I said he would see the Opera House after about one hundred* metres. He said thanks and *wanted to know why I spoke such good German/German so well.* *I explained that my parents had come here as immigrants from Germany 20 years ago.* So he *told me to tell them that I had met a Rainer from Schweinfurt.* I *said I would do that* before I said goodbye to him.

# Unit 1 — language B

## An experience in the outback

### 1 Grammar: If things had been different …

Which words on the right go well with the if-clauses on the left? Finish the sentences as in the example.

1. If Matt had grown up in the outback, [not take back] [Matt] [house]
   he would have learned to throw a boomerang.

2. If Jack hadn't grown up in the outback, [learn] [throw] [boomerang]
   he wouldn't have recognized the snake that bit Matt.

3. If the snake hadn't been poisonous, [Matt] [transport] [hospital]
   Jack would have laughed at his cousin.

4. If Jack's dad hadn't had a 4WD[1], [Jack] [laugh at] [cousin]
   they couldn't have taken Matt back to the house.

5. If the Flying Doctors hadn't got Jack's call, [not recognize] [snake] [Matt]
   Matt could not have been transported to hospital.

[1] 4WD = short for Four-Wheel-Drive – Geländewagen

### 2 Grammar: Which type of conditional?

Choose the right form to make conditional sentences.

1. If the weather is good tomorrow, …
   ✔ a) I will go to the beach.
   ☐ b) I would go to the beach.
   ☐ c) I would have gone to the beach.

2. I would have gone swimming every day …
   ☐ a) if I am not ill last week.
   ☐ b) if I wasn't ill last week.
   ✔ c) if I hadn't been ill last week.

3. If we lived in the north of Australia, …
   ☐ a) we can go surfing every day.
   ✔ b) we could go surfing every day.
   ☐ c) we could have gone surfing every day.

4. I would go surfing more often …
   ☐ a) if I don't have so much homework to do.
   ✔ b) if I didn't have so much homework to do.
   ☐ c) if I hadn't had so much homework to do.

5. If Sydney didn't have so many immigrants, …
   ☐ a) it will be a lot less interesting.
   ✔ b) it would be a lot less interesting.
   ☐ c) it would have been a lot less interesting.

6. I wouldn't be so nervous now …
   ☐ a) if I don't meet Lin yesterday.
   ☐ b) if I didn't meet Lin yesterday.
   ✔ c) if I hadn't met Lin yesterday.

### 3 Grammar: What if …?

Read the following text and make sentences to say what would / might / could happen or have happened if things were / had been different.

Be careful – some sentences are different from the basic types of conditionals.

Robert from Germany went on a working holiday to Australia for half a year in 2006.

1. Robert's English was good, so he wasn't worried.
   If Robert's English hadn't been so good, he might have been worried.

2. He didn't have to take the bus from Sydney Airport because he had met a nice boy on the plane.
   If he hadn't met a nice boy on the plane, he would have had to take the bus from Sydney Airport.

3. The boy's parents live in central Sydney, so they gave him a lift.
   If the boy's parents didn't live in central Sydney, they wouldn't have given him a lift.

4. When Robert told them the name of his hotel, they invited him to their house (it's a bad hotel).
   If Robert hadn't told them the name of his hotel, they wouldn't have invited him to their house.

5. Robert left after two weeks, because his new friend, Alex, had to go back to school.
   If his new friend Alex hadn't had to go back to school, Robert wouldn't have left after two weeks.

6. Alex's father, Mr Linsley, is a tourist guide, so he travels a lot.
   If Mr Linsley wasn't a tourist guide, he wouldn't travel so much.

7. Mr Linsley knows a lot of important people, so he was able to help Robert find a job.
   If Mr Linsley didn't know so many important people, he might not have been able to help Robert find a job.

8. Alex has the same hobbies as Robert so they still send each other e-mails.
   If Alex didn't have the same hobbies as Robert, they wouldn't still send each other e-mails.

### 4 Reading: How to 'make' water in the desert

a) Perhaps you know that koalas needn't drink water because they eat enough leaves from trees. Of course we humans do need water, but this doesn't mean we're lost if we forget to take enough of it on a trip in the Australian outback. Read the following instructions from an Australian survival handbook. Even though you probably do not know every single word, you should be able to understand the method that is described.

**How to to get water with the help of plastic sheeting[1]**
One of the ways of getting water in the bush is by using plastic sheeting. If you always carry a few pieces of heavy plastic, each about 1 m² in size, you will be able to collect about half a litre of water a day per sheet. In an emergency, any type of plastic – a raincoat or a bag – can be used.

**This is how to do it:** For each sheet, dig a hole in the ground, about 60 x 60 cm square and about 45 cm deep. Fill the bottom 10 cm of the hole with green leaves and branches from the trees around the place where you have set up camp; put a container of some sort in the middle – a cup is a bit too small!
Cover the hole with a plastic sheet and seal the edges with dirt to make it as airtight as possible.
In the middle of the sheet, place a stone heavy enough to make the plastic bulge towards the container.
With the heat of the sun, moisture[2] will slowly be drawn from the leaves and the ground, and will condense on the underside of the plastic. The water will then run down the slope made by the stone and drip into the container.

**Note:** The next day you must make the hole 3–4 cm deeper and put new leaves inside.

b) Nun fertige eine einfache Profilskizze an, die dir hilft, einem Freund oder einer Freundin das, was du soeben gelesen hast, zu erklären. Beschrifte sie auf Deutsch!

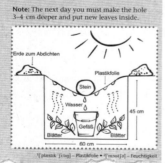

[1] ['plæstɪk 'ʃiːtɪŋ] – Plastikfolie • [2] ['mɔɪstʃə] – Feuchtigkeit

### 5 Listening: Weather forecasting

a) Listen to track 1 and choose the correct answer to the questions. b) Listen again and check your answers.

1. Barny works at a weather station in
   ☐ a) Austria.   ✔ b) Australia.

2. What's the weather like in Manchester?
   ✔ a) It's raining.   ☐ b) It isn't raining.

3. The sunniest capital in Australia is
   ☐ a) Sydney   ☐ b) Melbourne
   ✔ c) Darwin

4. How many hours of sunshine does Melbourne get?
   ☐ a) 5.5 hours   ☐ b) 6.7 hours
   ☐ c) 7.5 hours   ✔ d) 5.7 hours

5. On how many days of the year does it rain in Waratah?
   ☐ a) 214   ☐ b) 340
   ✔ c) 314

6. Snow falls in Australia above
   ✔ a) 1500 metres   ☐ b) 1300 metres
   ☐ c) 1600 metres

7. People visit the Australian Alps because the area is
   ☐ a) a natural park   ✔ b) a national park
   ☐ c) an international park

8. What's surprising? Canberra is
   ☐ a) the wettest city.   ☐ b) the cleanest city.
   ✔ c) the foggiest city.

### 6 Mediation: The outback

Lisa (15) ist mit ihren Eltern und ihrer 10-jährigen Schwester Clara zu Besuch auf einer Schaffarm im australischen Outback. Die beiden Mädchen sind auf einem Rundgang mit dem Sohn des Farmers und dessen Hund. Da Jeff (16) kein Deutsch und Clara kaum Englisch spricht, muss Lisa für die beiden dolmetschen. Benutze if-Sätze in Lisas Übertragungen.

*Clara:* Wir müssen jetzt wieder zurück, sonst fahren Mama und Papa ohne uns ab.

*Lisa:* She says if we don't go back now, Mum and Dad will leave without us.

*Jeff:* Well, if you hadn't wanted to go so far out, we wouldn't have to hurry now.

*Lisa:* Er sagt, wenn wir nicht hätten so weit raus gehen wollen, müssten wir uns jetzt nicht beeilen.

*Clara:* Gut, dass wir den Hund dabei haben, sonst würden wir nie zum Haus zurückfinden.

*Lisa:* She says if we didn't have the dog with us, we'd never find our way back to the house.

*Jeff:* Rubbish! I wouldn't have taken you girls out here if our lives had depended on my old dog.

*Lisa:* Er sagt, er hätte uns nicht mit hier herausgenommen, wenn unser Leben von seinem alten Hund abhängen würde.

*Clara:* Wenn ich euch sagen müsste, wo das Haus ist, hätte ich keine Chance.

*Lisa:* She says if she had to tell us where the house is, she wouldn't have a chance.

*Jeff:* Well, if you'd lived here for more than ten years, you would know where to go, too.

*Lisa:* Er sagt, wenn wir hier seit mehr als zehn Jahren leben würden, wüssten wir auch, wohin wir (gehen) müssten.

*Clara:* Unmöglich! Und außerdem – wenn er mir vorher gesagt hätte, dass hier alles gleich aussieht, wäre ich gar nicht mitgekommen.

*Lisa:* She says that's *impossible*! And if you'd told her that everything looked the same out here, she wouldn't have come with us (at all).

*Jeff:* Well, if she had asked me, I would have told her. Tell her to watch out for snakes and crocodiles on the way back.

*Lisa:* Er sagt, wenn du ihn gefragt hättest, hätte er es dir gesagt. Außerdem meint er, du sollst auf dem Rückweg auf Schlangen und Krokodile achten!

*Clara:* Aaaaaah!

# Unit 1 — Rabbit-proof fence

## 1 Cloze test: How the kangaroo got its tail (based on an Australian Aboriginal legend)

Complete the text with suitable words.

A long **time** ago, Kareela the Kangaroo and Wambiri the Wombat lived **together** in a hut. They liked being with **each** other, but Kareela liked **to** sleep outside at night and he **made** fun of Wambiri, who always **wanted** to sleep inside. "Come on, Wambiri, **sleep** outside with me," said Kareela. "It's much nicer to **look** up at the stars at night and listen to the fresh wind in the trees." "It's too **cold** outside," said Wambiri, "and sometimes it **rains**. I might **get** wet! I like sleeping in my hut with a nice fire to keep me warm." When winter came, the wind **got/became** colder at night. At first Kareela didn't **mind**. He **told** himself that the wind couldn't **hurt** him – he wasn't afraid. When it **started** to rain, he said "a little wind and rain **can't/won't** hurt me. I'm not afraid." But one night, Kareela was so **wet** and cold, he **couldn't** take it any longer. He got up and **knocked** on Wambiri's door. "It's me!" screamed Kareela. "Now, **let** me in!" "No!" shouted Wambiri. "There isn't **enough** room." Kareela became very **angry** and pushed hard at the **door** until it opened. "I'm **inside** now – and you aren't big enough to **throw/kick** me out!" – "Well, sleep **over** there – in the corner," said Wambiri and **went** back to sleep near the fire. Kareela **lay** down in the corner, but **there** was a hole in the wall of the **hut** and the wind and rain came in. He couldn't dry **himself** or get warm. In the **morning** he felt terrible. He went outside and **picked** up a large rock. Wambiri was just **getting/waking** up when Kareela dropped the **rock** on his head. "That's for **not** helping me get warm and dry," said Kareela. "And **from** now on, you'll always **live** in a cold, dark hole." After that, Wambiri and Kareela didn't **talk** to each other or play together, and Wambiri planned his **revenge**. He made a big spear and **waited** until Kareela was washing **himself**. Then he **threw** the spear, and it **hit** the kangaroo at the base of his spine[1]. Kareela screamed in pain and tried to **pull** the spear out, but he couldn't. "From now on, that **will** be your long tail," shouted Wambiri, "and you'll **never** have a home to live in!" That is **why** wombats now have flat foreheads[2] and live in dark, damp burrows[3] and why kangaroos have long **tails** and always sleep outside, under the stars.

[1] [spaɪn] – Steißbein • [2] [ˈfɔrɪd] – Stirn • [3] [ˌdæmp ˈbʌrəʊ] – feuchter Bau

## 2 Listening: Gold-mining in Western Australia

a) Before listening to track 2 look at these words and their definitions.

**Gold-mining** is going underground to find gold.
**Gold fields** are places where you can find gold in the ground.
**Grasslands** are places to keep cattle.
**The Gold Rush** was when a lot of people from Australia and other parts of the world went to look for gold.
An **ounce** of gold is about 31 grams.
A **claim** is registered by someone who finds gold and says that they want to look for more at one certain place.
A **pipeline** is a long pipe to transport water or oil a long way.
A **mile** is 1.6 kilometres.

b) Now complete the puzzle with the words above. There are no spaces between the words.

1. Where farmers keep their cattle in Australia.
2. This is made by someone who finds gold somewhere and wants people to know he was there first.
3. This was what happened when a lot of people went to find gold.
4. A way of measuring how far away a place is.
5. This carries water from a reservoir to a town or city.
6. This is where people found gold.
7. 31 grams of gold are about an … of gold.
8. The name of the metal in the puzzle.

Puzzle answers: GRASSLANDS, CLAIM, GOLDRUSH, MILE, PIPELINE, GOLDFIELDS, OUNCE, GOLD

c) Listen to track 2 twice. Here are some of the numbers the text talks about. Decide if the definition of each number is true or false.

| | | | true | false |
|---|---|---|---|---|
| 1. | 1863 | The first man rode over the gold fields in Western Australia. | ✓ | |
| 2. | 1864–68 | A man named C.C. Hunt crossed the gold fields. | ✓ | |
| 3. | 500–1000 | This much money in pounds was given to the last person to find gold. | | ✓ |
| 4. | 554 | This is the amount of gold in ounces found in a town called Coolgardie. | ✓ | |
| 5. | 1893 | Three Irishmen started looking for gold in Western Australia. | ✓ | |
| 6. | 1903 | A pipeline brought oil to the gold-miners. | | ✓ |
| 7. | 557 | The length of the pipeline in miles. | | ✓ |
| 8. | 35,000,000 | The weight of gold in ounces found in Kalgoorlie gold mines since 1893. | ✓ | |

d) Listen again and check your answers. If you got them all right first time, that's very good!

---

# Unit 1 — let's check

## 1 Reading: Christmas down under

Complete the text – as shown in line 1 – with the words below.

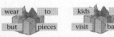  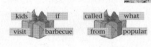  

wear — to — kids — if — called — what — cards — it — until
but — pieces — visit — barbecue — from — popular — so — never — box

Australians celebrate Christmas, too, but **it** is very different **from** Christmas in Europe or North America. Of course Christmas down under is **never** white, especially as it is in summer. Temperatures are about 25 to 38 degrees Celcius, **so** most Australians have their parties outdoors, for example with a real Australian **barbecue**! Picnics on the beach are very **popular**, too, and it is great to see **what** Aussies take down to the beach on Christmas Day: whole turkeys, huge **pieces** of ham, large bowls of salad, cakes, puddings and at least one esky, a large plastic **box** to keep drinks cool, per person. Santa Claus doesn't **visit** Australia on a sleigh that is pulled by reindeer, he comes on a surfboard that is pulled by six white kangaroos which are **called** 'boomers'! And of course it is much too hot to **wear** a coat, so Santa has a red T-shirt and shorts on! For Australian Christmas is the best time of the year not only because they get presents, **but** also because it's the time of their longest holidays, which last six weeks **until** the end of January. But there are things which are very similar to Christmas in Europe or North America. Children write **cards** letters to Santa Claus with the things they would like to have. Many people go **to** church on Christmas Eve. People put up Christmas decorations, and many families have a 'Christmas tree' – even **if** it's only a branch from a gumtree[1]!

[1] [ˈɡʌmtriː] – Eukalyptusbaum

## 2 C-test: Rabbit-proof fence   Complete the missing words.

First the sound of the plane r**eminded** Daisy of the Flying Doctors, who came to her village three or four t**imes** a year. But when she saw that it was c**ircling** above them, she knew it meant d**anger**, because the people in it were probably l**ooking** down to find three little r**unaway** girls. Planes were much worse than all the s**earch** parties with dogs and horses. They had to follow their f**ootsteps**, which had been washed away by the rain. But from the **air** they were easy to see, because in the d**esert** there were large areas without any t**rees** and it was impossible to find s**helter**. But this time they **were** lucky – there were some big trees straight **ahead** of them, so they ran, climbed up and h**id** under the branches. After some minutes, the plane **gave** up, and the girls walked on in s**ilence**.

---

# Focus on the Golden Age

## 1 Reading: The Spanish Armada

It was a hot evening in July, 1588. All was quiet in Plymouth harbour where the English ships <u>lay</u> at <u>anchor</u>. Everybody, however, knew it was the <u>calm</u> before the storm because the Great Armada was waiting to attack England. On that evening Sir Francis Drake and a few other officers had gone to play bowls when the news was brought that the Spanish ships had been <u>spotted</u> in the English Channel.

Drake had a plan in mind, but he wanted to finish the game he was playing before he put his plan into action. He let the 130 huge Spanish ships with 30,000 men on board sail up the Channel before attacking them from the <u>rear</u>. Then the British ships, only half the size of the Spanish ones, <u>fired</u> their guns and turned away quickly before the enemy could return the fire.

Eventually the Spanish <u>cast</u> anchor just off Calais, a place they thought to be safe. But Drake knew how to force them out to sea again: The British filled their ships with <u>pitch</u>, set fire to them and let them <u>drift</u> towards the Spanish, who cut their ropes and sailed off in great chaos. A <u>fierce</u> storm drove them north to Scotland and Ireland where most of the ships were lost in heavy seas. Only fifty-four of them returned to Spain.

a) Use your dictionary to find the correct meaning of the underlined words.

| Word in the text | Dictionary | German |
|---|---|---|
| lay | vi: to lie — lay — lain | liegen — lag — gelegen |
| anchor | s | Anker |
| calm | s | Ruhe |
| spotted | vt: to spot sb/sth | entdecken |
| rear | s | hinten |
| fired | vt: to fire — fired — fired | feuern — feuerte — gefeuert |
| cast | vt: to cast — cast — cast | werfen |
| pitch | s | Pech |
| drift | vi: to drift | treiben |
| fierce | adj | heftig, zerstörerisch |

b) Find synonyms for these words in the text.

| eventually – **finally, in the end, at last** |
| cast – **dropped** |
| off – **near** |

c) Find opposites from the text.

| tiny – **huge** |
| front – **rear** |
| gentle – **fierce** |

# focus 1

## 2 Vocabulary: Guess who I am

All these people lived between 1400 and 1600. They give you a clue so that you can guess who they are.

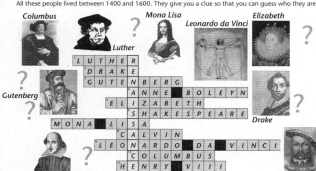

1. I think people should live according to the moral values of the Bible.
2. I'm from Devon and I sailed around the world in my ship "The Golden Hinde".
3. I'm German and I invented the printing press.
4. Once I was Queen, but I was executed when my husband wanted to take a new wife.
5. I never married because I wanted to serve my country as Queen.
6. I'm good at writing drama and poems. I hope my Queen likes it.
7. I'm an Italian lady in a famous picture.
8. I think there is too much ceremony in the Catholic church, we should have some changes.
9. I painted the famous picture of the Italian lady.
10. I wanted to find a new route to India, but actually landed at the other side of the world.
11. I'm the king who married six times to have a son, but in the end my daughter became Queen.

## 3 Vocabulary: Word families

a) Make adjectives from these nouns.

| gold | *golden* |
| wealth | *wealthy* |
| value | *valuable* |
| poison | *poisonous* |
| crowd | *crowded* |
| danger | *dangerous* |
| death | *dead, deadly* |

b) Make nouns from these verbs.

| to settle | *settler, settlement* |
| to speak | *speaker, speech* |
| to influence | *influence* |
| to sail | *sailor* |
| to colonize | *colony, colonist* |
| to print | *printer* |
| to explore | *explorer* |

---

# On the southwestern coast — unit 2 intro

## 1 Vocabulary: Crossword puzzle

**Down**
1. A Devon town with a famous cathedral.
2. A small bay.
3. A place where ghosts are believed to be is …
5. A town near Land's End.
7. A person who visits interesting places.
8. Here you find a museum of smuggling.
9. Something you can find on the "Jurassic Coast".
12. A drink produced in Devon.

**Across**
4. The port Sir Francis Drake sailed from against the Armada.
6. King Arthur's legendary birthplace.
10. The Gulf Stream makes the … in Cornwall mild.
11. Wild ponies live here.
13. The south coast of Cornwall is called the "English …".

## Paradise on earth — language A

### 1 Grammar: On Saturday at 11 o'clock in Torquay

Write what is happening in the pictures. Use passive forms in the present progressive.

1. Fruit and vegetables _are being sold_ (sell) at the market.
2. Boats _are being pushed_ (push) into the sea.
3. Sails _are being put up_ (put up) by two young men.
4. Restaurant tables _are being set_ (set) for lunch.
5. Mrs Pierce _is being asked_ (ask) the way by a tourist.

An hour later: Write passive sentences in the present perfect.

1. Most of the fruit _has been sold_.
2. The boats _have been pushed_ into the water. They are out at sea now.
3. The sails _have been put up_ and the two men have sailed away.
4. The tables _have been set_ and the first guests have arrived.
5. The tourist's questions _have been answered_ and Mrs Pierce has gone home.

---

# unit 2 — language A

## 2 Speaking: Visiting the Eden Project

Tobias and Edith, two German pupils who are doing a two-week language course at a language school near Exeter are visiting the Eden Project. They are asking a guide about the project. Write the guide's answers in the correct tense. Use passive forms.

1. **Is it true that people call the Eden project a world wonder?**
Yes, it _is sometimes (has sometimes been) referred to_ (sometimes • refer to) as the eighth wonder of the world.

2. **Where did the money for the project come from?**
Well, most of the project _was paid for_ (pay for) with lottery money, but part of it _has been/was earned_ (earn) from visitors like you.

3. **I've heard that they made a James Bond movie here in Eden.**
That's true. "The other day" with Pierce Brosnan _was filmed_ (film) here.

4. **Where did you get the plants from?**
Actually, most of the plants _were grown_ (grow) from seeds and not _taken_ (take) from the wild.

5. **What exactly does the Eden Project want the visitors to learn?**
Well, the visitors _are (being) taught_ (teach) here about the natural world. They _are shown_ (show) how natural resources _have to be saved_ (have to • save) so that they _can be used_ (can • use) in the future.

6. **Could you tell us how you use the rain water that falls on the roof?**
Of course it is _used_ (use) to water the plants, and the mist _is created_ (create) with it. But also the toilets _are flushed_ (flush) with it.

7. **We've seen so many buses outside. What do you do when there are too many visitors?**
That's really a problem. Once or twice our gates _have been closed_ (close) so that visitors had to wait to _be let in_ (let in).

## 3 Vocabulary: Working with the dictionary

Take your dictionary and find out how the words on the right can be used.

contain, display, refer to, environment, label, remove, Mediterranean, humid, damage, resources, rare, seed

1. Four words can be nouns and verbs: display, _label, damage, seed_
2. Two words are only adjectives: _humid, rare_
3. Which words are only nouns? _environment, resources_
4. Which words are only verbs? _refer to, contain, remove_
5. Which word can be an adjective and a noun? _Mediterranean_

---

# unit 2 — language A

## 4 Grammar: After the storm

Mr Burton was away in London when the storm hit his little village at the seaside.
Use the past progressive form of the passive to describe what was being done, when he got home.

1. An old man _was being carried_ (carry) into an ambulance.
2. A little boy _was being examined_ (examine) by a doctor, while his brother, who was still missing, _was being looked for_ (look for) by some village people.
3. Some chairs _were being taken back_ (take back) to the café.
4. A big tree _was being removed_ (remove) from the street.
5. A damaged car _was being towed_ (tow) to the garage to be repaired.
6. Photos _were being taken_ (take) by a photographer and his neighbour _was being interviewed_ (interview) by a journalist.

## Two men in a boat — language B

### 1 Grammar: At the tourist office

Susan works at the tourist office in Penzance. People come to her with their questions and problems. Change their statements by using the personal passive.

- **Somebody told me that there is a bus to Land's End. Can you tell me where it leaves from?**
_I was told_ that there is a bus to Land's End. Can you tell me where it leaves from?

- **Nobody told us that there is a rock concert near our hotel on Saturday. Do you think we can move to another hotel?**
_We weren't told_ that there is a rock concert near our hotel on Saturday. Do you think we can move to another hotel?

- **Someone asked me if I want to go to the rock concert with him. Do you know where I can buy a ticket?**
_I was asked_ if I want to go to the rock concert. Do you know where I can buy a ticket?

- **Nobody gave me the list of the local hotels when I arrived. Could I have one, please?**
_I wasn't given_ the list of the local hotels when I arrived. Could I have one, please?

# unit 2 language B

## 2 Reading: The Dartmoor pony

a) Read the text and look up the unknown words in your dictionary. Then fill in the grid with suitable words from the text.

| activities | pony | attributes |
|---|---|---|
| ride, | Dartmoor pony, | hearty, |
| breed, | stallion, | sturdy, |
| roam, | mare, | robust, |
| needed for | foal, | dark in colour, |
| farm work, | warm blood | white markings, |
| live outside, | (type), | true to type |
| carry tin | breed | |

b) Read the text again and put in the correct verb forms, active or passive.

Dartmoor ponies are often dark in colour; white markings, if any, are very small. As a hearty moorland breed they are sturdy and similar to a warm blood type. The Dartmoor pony **was first mentioned** (first • mention) in a text from the Middle Ages. Much later, in the 19th century, at the height of tin mining[1] on Dartmoor, the ponies **were used** (use) for carrying the tin from the mines. When this finished, they **were left** (leave) to roam free apart from those that **were needed** (need) for work around the farms. Until the 1960s quite a number of them **were ridden** (ride) by the warders[2] of Dartmoor prison as they **took** (take) prisoners to and from their work outside.

During the last twenty years special programmes **have been started** (start) to interest farmers in breeding a true to type Dartmoor pony, robust enough to live outside on Dartmoor all the year round. Here is one example: About ten mares **were chosen** (choose) for breeding and **were turned out** (turn out) in a special place with a Dartmoor stallion. Before that the old stone walls around the fields **had to be put up** (must • put up) again and also new fences **were built** (build). During the early autumn the mares **were collected** (collect) and **returned** (return) to their owners, the foals **were taken** (take) to a warmer place. The following year, the programme **was continued** (continue) with another group of mares and stallions.

[1] ['tɪn ˌmaɪnɪŋ] – Zinnbergbau • [2] ['wɔːdə] – Wärter(in)

## 3 Reading: Letterboxing

a) Steffi from Regensburg is on a trip to Dartmoor with Mr Cocker, their language school teacher, who has organised a letterboxing activity for his group. Read the information about letterboxing on Dartmoor.

Dartmoor with its beautiful landscape has been a National Park since 1951. Although it is the home of a lot of typical plants and wildlife, people are allowed to go horseback riding and hiking on the open land. Walking tours are very popular with people of all age groups. They go and look at the great many tors[1] of all shapes and sizes, listen to the ghost stories told about them or they take part in letterboxing, an outdoor activity where people have to find their way across the country with the help of a map and compass[2].

**Rules for letterboxing.**
- Don't damage the land.
- Put the box back exactly as you found it.
- Do not take risks.
- Follow the rules.
- Close all gates after use.
- Keep to paths across farmland.
- Leave no rubbish.
- Protect wildlife, wild plants and trees.

The letterbox is a small pot with a stamp[3] and a visitors' book in it. You have to find it and read the clue that leads you to another letterbox. Then you make a copy of the stamp and write your name in the visitors' book.

Oh, I know, it's a bit like a game we play, it's called *Schnitzeljagd*.

[1] [tɔː] – typische Felsblöcke in Dartmoor • [2] ['kʌmpəs] – Kompass • [3] [stæmp] – Stempel

b) In the evening Steffi told her host family about her interesting day on Dartmoor. Write down what she said using the personal passive. Use each of the following words once.

take   tell   show   give   remind   ask   warn

1. Today **we were taken** to Dartmoor and **given** a brochure about letterboxing.
2. **We were told not** to damage the land and keep to the paths.
3. **We were reminded** to follow the rules and put the box back exactly as we had found it.
4. **We were warned not** to take any risks.
5. **We were shown** how to close the gates after use.
6. **We were asked** to leave no rubbish and protect wild plants and animals.

---

# unit 2 text

## The ghost of St Dominic

### 1 Grammar: What the police had to find out

In 1720, after Captain Parfitt's ship had sunk, the local police had a lot of questions. Ask the questions they had to find answers to. Be careful! Some are in the passive!

1. When exactly **did the ship sink** (the ship • sink)?
2. What **happened/has happened to the crew** (happen • to the crew)?
3. How many **sailors drowned** (sailors • drown)?
4. If anybody survived, where **did they go/have they gone** (they • go)?
5. Where **was the cargo taken/has the cargo been taken** (cargo • take)?
6. Why **did the ship end up in the little cove** (the ship • end up • in the little cove)?
7. Who **was the fire made by** (the fire • make • by)?
8. Who **did the wreckers sell the cargo to** (the wreckers • sell • to • cargo)?

### 2 Writing: The latest news

Mr Saunders, who is almost deaf in one ear, heard people talking in the village shop. Now he's telling his neighbour, Mrs Curtis, the latest news. Correct what he said.

1. There's a young man in the vicar's house who has come from a hospital in France.
2. He's called Jim Nodd and he's spending a few weeks with his uncle, the Reverend Bellows.
3. The reverend is mean to him. He makes him work hard and doesn't feed him well.
4. At first Jack felt lonely because his uncle was always working. So he started to visit the fishing villages along the coast.
5. He's made friends with Rebecca, the housekeeper's wife
6. Sometimes they sit in the church where Rebecca tells him stories from the bible.

1. There's a young man in the vicar's house who has come from an orphanage in London.
2. He's called Jack Todd and he has come to live with his uncle, the Reverend Bellows.
3. The reverend is generous to him. Jack only has to do little jobs around the house and is given plenty to eat.
4. He felt lonely because he missed his friends from the orphanage. But then he got to know Rebecca.
5. He's made friends with Rebecca, the housekeeper's daughter.
6. Sometimes they sit in front of the kitchen fire where she tells him stories about Cornwall.

### 3 Listening: Booking a ghost tour in London

a) Listen to track 3, then choose the correct answer to the questions. b) Listen again to check your answers.

| | | | |
|---|---|---|---|
| 1. How many people want to go on the ghost tour? | ☐ 10 | ✓ 12 | ☐ 11 |
| 2. How many different tours are there? | ☐ 2 | ✓ 3 | ☐ 4 |
| 3. What is Mrs Oldfield's husband's first name? | ✓ Peter | ☐ Dieter | ☐ Richard |
| 4. When is Halloween? | ☐ October 30th | ✓ October 31st | ☐ November 1st |
| 5. How long does the Halloween tour take? | ☐ one hour | ☐ one and a half hours | ✓ two hours |
| 6. Who is the guide on the ghost tour? | ☐ the men in black | ✓ the woman in black | ☐ a woman in white |
| 7. Mrs Oldfield doesn't want to go on the ghost tour. Why? What do you think? | ☐ She has no money. | ☐ She doesn't play football. | ✓ She's scared. |

### 4 Listening: Cornish ghosts

a) Before you listen to track 4, look at this information:

What does a dog do when it is pleased? It **wags** its tail.
A **ghost-hunter** is somebody who goes to old places to look for ghosts.

b) Choose the right answers to complete the sentences. Listen again and check your answers.

1. Margot Murphy talks about ghosts in
   a) Scotland.
   ✓ b) Cornwall.
   c) London.

2. The name of the hotel in Boscastle is
   ✓ a) the Wellington Hotel.
   b) the Jamaica Inn.
   c) the Napoleon Hotel.

3. The ghost seen by the owner of the Wellington Hotel
   a) jumped from the roof.
   b) went to bed.
   ✓ c) walked through the wall.

4. The ghost at the Dolphin Inn in Penzance was
   a) a farmer.
   b) a waiter.
   ✓ c) a sailor.

5. The ghost at the Dolphin Inn was sitting
   a) on a chair.
   ✓ b) on a wall.
   c) in a boat.

6. The name of the ghost at the house in Duport was
   ✓ a) Flo.
   b) Rose.
   c) Nora.

7. The ghost seen by the five-year-old granddaughter was wearing
   a) a black coat.
   b) a blue coat.
   ✓ c) a black dress.

8. What does a ghost do when it wants to leave a room?
   a) It opens a cupboard.
   ✓ b) It walks through a wall.
   c) It sits on a wall.

## 5 Mediation: Piracy¹ today

**a)** Read the following text. Remember that you needn't understand every word.

Piracy has been a problem in the southeast Asian seas for centuries and is becoming an increasing threat² to global trade. Nearly two-thirds of all worldwide attacks happen in Asia, most of them taking place in Indonesia's waters and ports.
Sometimes the ships are boarded and hijacked³ on the high seas, but more often the ships are attacked while they are lying in a port. The targets of an attack are usually parts of the ship's loads, its safe and its crew's valuables. Stealing a whole ship or its complete cargo on the high seas makes only a small part of the reported crimes. Almost all reported acts of piracy are done by armed pirates who threaten⁴ and often injure, kidnap, or kill some of the crew.
Today's pirates may be normal fishermen, gangsters, and sometimes even local police. The fact that most attacks happen while a ship is in port or anchored near the coast makes it very probable that some of the police in this region could have something to do with these crimes. Usually the pirates are heavily armed men with military-style weapons; in some cases they were reported to have worn army uniforms and masks.
What might be the reasons for somebody to become a pirate? It is widely known that the economic crisis has made a lot of men lose their jobs so that they can no longer earn enough money to feed their families. Even the police are underpaid, and the military often do not pay their officers and soldiers enough money either which means that a lot of corruption has developed in a number of countries. And for someone working in the police or the army it is easy to get hold of the arms and instruments necessary for hijacking a ship.

¹['paɪərəsɪ] – Piraterie, Seeräuberei • ²[θret] – Bedrohung • ³['haɪdʒæk] – kapern • ⁴['θretn] – bedrohen

**b)** This is part of a report that students from different countries have just been given at their language school. Florian didn't listen carefully so he'll have to ask his neighbour what exactly the report was about. He has collected his questions in German. Write the dialogue between Florian and Mike. The verbs may be active or passive.

1. Ist Seeräuberei ein neues Problem in Südostasien?
2. Warum schreiben die Zeitungen häufig darüber?
3. Wo werden die Schiffe überfallen?
4. Was wird normalerweise gestohlen?
5. Werden Menschen bei den Überfällen verletzt?
6. Wer sind die Piraten?
7. Warum wird jemand zum Pirat?
8. Woher bekommen die Piraten moderne Waffen?

*Florian:* Is piracy a new problem in southeast Asia?

*Mike:* No, not really, it has been a problem for centuries.

*Florian:* Why do newspapers often report it?

*Mike:* Well, it is becoming/has become a bigger and bigger risk on the seas.

*Florian:* Where are (the) ships attacked?

*Mike:* Sometimes the ships are attacked/boarded and hijacked on the high seas, but quite often it happens in the ports, too.

*Florian:* What is usually stolen?

*Mike:* The pirates are mostly interested in parts of the ship's load/cargo, the safe and the crew's valuables. Very rarely whole ships or cargoes are stolen.

*Florian:* Do people get injured/Are people hurt in the attacks?

*Mike:* Yes, they are. Very often the crew are threatened, injured, kidnapped or even killed.

*Florian:* Who are the pirates?

*Mike:* Actually, all sorts of people can be pirates. They may be normal fishermen, gangsters, or people who have lost their jobs or even the local police, which is highly probable because most attacks happen/take place in the ports.

*Florian:* Why does somebody become a pirate?

*Mike:* There are very many poor people in this region and a lot of men have families who have to be fed. What can they do when they have no work? Even the police and the soldiers do not earn enough money.

*Florian:* Where do the pirates get modern weapons from?

*Mike:* There is quite a lot of corruption in these countries, you know. So weapons might be bought from soldiers or the police, if they themselves do not take part in the crimes anyway.

## On the southwestern coast

### 1 Grammar: The Magic¹ Wizzix

Mr Laziman believes in everything that is modern, so he bought a Magic Wizzix on the Internet some weeks ago. But after four weeks he was really annoyed. Mr Laziman talked to his neighbour Mrs Bisibee.

**A fantastic cleaner!**
Your rooms have never been so clean! **Cleans the air:** Your rooms won't smell of dogs anymore. **Moves around** easily! Magic Wizzix works wonders! Magic Wizzix's **magic broom²** cleans walls and ceilings. Just mount³ the broom and push. Magic Wizzix does all you want by itself. It's just magic!
**Excellent service!** Any problem? Call us or write an e-mail, we'll be there to help you at once.

"I was really happy to have my new Magic Wizzix, but then things began to go wrong. I'm sure, I did everything just as ___I was told___ (tell). ___I was promised___ (promise) that it would move around the room easily, but then when I left it to work alone it bumped into my television and broke it. ___I was told___ (tell) that it can remove the smell

¹['mædʒɪk] – magisch • ²[bruːm] – Besen • ³[maʊnt] – aufbauen; aufsteigen

of dogs. Could I borrow your dog to test if it's true? ___I was informed___ (inform) that I could mount its broom and play a game of Quidditch⁴. So I opened the window, stood on the kitchen table and climbed onto the broom. But when I switched my Wizzix on, it didn't take me up into the air. Instead I fell from the table and hurt my foot. There was a big spot⁵ on my wall in the living room, you know. I ___'ve been advised___ (advise) by my son not to mount the broom again to clean the wall. Maybe I'll fall off again. I have already written an e-mail to the company, but ___I haven't been given___ (not give) an answer yet. Look here, Mrs Bisibee, ___I've been offered___ (offer) help at any time of the day. But when I ring this number, it's always engaged. Can't you help me?"

⁴a ride on a broom in Harry Potter • ⁵[spɒt] – Fleck

### 2 Grammar: Helpful Mrs Bisibee

Of course, Mrs Bisibee was able to help her neighbour. She had been waiting for her chance to help and didn't stop talking when Mr Laziman asked her for help. Use conditional sentences.

"Of course, I'll help you, Mr Laziman. If I'd read about the Magic Wizzix, I ___wouldn't have trusted___ (not trust) those promises. If you ___buy___ (buy) something on the Internet, you never know whether you can give it back. If I ___were___ (be) you, I ___'d write___ (write) a letter to the company and complain. But wouldn't it be a good idea, if you ___showed___ (show) me your Wizzix first. I ___could try___ (can try) and help, if you let me in. … Oh dear, is that the spot you wanted to clean? If you really ___want___ (want) the wall to be clean again, you must … Oh, actually, I can clean it for you, if you ___make___ (make) us a nice cup of tea. Tell me, Mr Laziman, do you really believe in magic? If somebody else had told me your story, I ___wouldn't have believed___ (not believe) it. Never mind, if you ___haven't got___ (not have got) any tea at home, come over to my place. You know, if you ___are___ (be) interested in Quidditch, we could go to the cinema together. We could watch the new Harry Potter film, if you ___like___ (like). I ___'d be___ (be) very pleased if you'd spend the evening with me. Come on, if we ___don't hurry___ (not hurry) up, we'll be late for the film."

## Units 1+2 revision

### 1 Reading: A legend from Devon

Complete the text with these words as shown in line 1.

about • an • appeared • arms • at • called • did • down • Everybody • haunting • left • of • on • On • out • put • sad • story • terribly • the • to • until • was • was • was • when • who

Long ago, back in the 17th century, a young woman |Anne
                                                  called
Taylor lived near a little Exmoor town. As with many legends,
her| is about two men|loved the same woman. One of them,
   story             who
John Howard, was very jealous, and it was him who she|in
                                                     left
the end. Of course he was. Day after day he thought|his lost
                                              sad           about
love and he began to hate Anne. At last the day came|Anne and
                                                     when
the new man in her life decided to get married. It did not take
long|John got the news, too.
     until
He felt|hurt and sank into a deep silence. On|day of their wedding¹ her future husband stood waiting
       terribly                              the
at the altar with a loving smile|his face. After the ceremony husband and wife walked|the church
                                 on                                                   down
and stepped outside. Suddenly a loud bang|heard. For a moment it was as if time had stood still,
                                          was
nobody moved and nobody spoke.|looked in shock|the body of Anne Taylor. Her white dress|covered
                              Everybody        at                                        was
in the blood which slowly came|of a small hole over her heart. Her husband got on his knees beside her
                               out
and took her small lifeless body in his|with tears running down his face. It was as if he|trying to put her
                                        arms                                              was
to sleep.

Legend does not say what happened to Anne's
killer, but if there is any truth in|event of 1965, her
                                    an
soul is still|the place. In that year a young woman
              haunting
was going|get married in the same church.|the
          to                               On
morning of the wedding a young woman wearing a
17th century wedding dress|to a guest just outside
                           appeared
his room. Luckily the bride² of 1965|not take this
                                     did
to be a bad sign and went ahead with the wedding.
It is said that she|her bridal bouquet³ on the grave|
                    put                              of
Anne Taylor as a symbol of respect.

¹['wedɪŋ] – Hochzeit • ²[braɪd] – Braut • ³['braɪdl bʊ'keɪ] – Brautstrauß

# Unit 3 intro: Young people in Scotland

## 1 Mixed bag: Three teenagers

While Florian was travelling through Scotland with his parents, he met three very different teenagers. Use the following words to connect the sentences.

| however | which | in order to | although | whose | when | because | apart from | like | as |
| since | who | and | also | instead of | although | in fact | which | where | who |

Amir, _whose_ parents own a corner shop in Glasgow, is a great Celtic fan. _Although_ he has to work hard for school, he sometimes helps in the shop _when_ he wants to earn some money. He needs it for football tickets and _also_ for another expensive hobby: CDs and concerts. _As_ there are so many rock groups in Glasgow, he sometimes can't decide _which_ concert to go to. But in the end he always finds a friend _who_ wants to go with him and then they decide together.

Emma, _who_ he met at the bed and breakfast place _where_ they spent their first night in the Highlands, is a totally different person. _Since_ she lives quite a long way from her school, _in fact_ right at the southern end of Loch Ness, she is picked up by a bus every morning _which_ takes her to school. _Although_ there is not much to do in her part of Scotland, she doesn't feel bored. _Like_ her friend Hazel she speaks with a strong Scottish accent.

Mark, _however_, doesn't have a Scottish accent, as he is from England _and_ has lived in Scotland for only a year. They moved to Aberdeen _because_ his father was given a job on an oil rig. _Apart from_ some typically Scottish traditions, Mark doesn't find life in Scotland so very different. _Instead of_ going to pop concerts, some people here like to go to a ceilidh from time to time _in order to_ enjoy dancing, singing and listening to stories.

## 2 Vocabulary: Countries and their people

| country | people | nationality |
|---|---|---|
| Spain | Spaniard, the Spanish (pl.) | Spanish |
| Britain | Briton, the British (pl.) | British |
| England | Englishman, Englishwoman, the English (pl.) | English |
| Scotland | Scot, Scotsman, Scotswoman, the Scots (pl.) | Scottish |
| Ireland | Irishman, Irishwoman, the Irish (pl.) | Irish |
| France | Frenchman, Frenchwoman, the French (pl.) | French |

---

# Unit 3 language A: Please, Dad!

## 1 Speaking: Dialogues

Complete the dialogues with phrases from the box. Learn the sentences by heart. They contain some important phrases with the indefinite article.

> 24 hours a day • in a hurry • quite a long way • for a change • a pity • six days a week • rather an interesting new game • quarter of an hour ago • an American • a headache • two and a half hours • 55p a piece • 90p a kilo • a software designer • three times a week • a silly idea

**1.** *Mrs McArthur:* Brian's mother? She's _a software designer_ in Edinburgh.
*Mrs McDonald:* Do you think she has time for a cup of tea?
*Mrs McArthur:* I'm not sure. She's _always in a hurry_ because she has to travel to her firm _three times a week_.
*Mrs McDonald:* I see. That's _quite a long way_. Is she Scottish?
*Mrs McArthur:* No, I think she's _an American_, but her husband is Scottish.

**2.** *Mike:* Hi Brian. Would you like to come out and play football with us?
*Brian:* No, sorry. I'm ill. I've got _a headache_.
*Mike:* What _a pity_! Let's play cards _for a change_. I know _rather an interesting new game_.
*Brian:* _What a silly idea!_ We're not babies!

**3.** *Mr Wilson:* Could I talk to your dad, please?
*David:* Sorry, he left _quarter of an hour ago_.
*Mr Wilson:* OK. I'll call again in _two and a half hours_.

**4.** *Customer:* When do you close for the night?
*Owner:* We're open _24 hours a day_.
*Customer:* Are you open every day?
*Owner:* No, only _six days a week_. We're closed on Mondays.
*Customer:* How much are the apples?
*Owner:* They're _90p a kilo_.
*Customer:* And that chocolate cake?
*Owner:* Oh, that's _55p a piece_.

---

# Unit 3 language A

## 2 Grammar: Florian's letter

Put a tick (✔) in the box when the *definite article* is needed.

Dear Patrick,
We almost missed ✔ B&B, when we drove up from ☐ Loch Ness last night. ✔ Campbells live in such a sweet little house. Mrs Campbell gave us a warm welcome and offered us a cup of ☐ tea. She didn't invite us for ☐ tea though because they only do ☐ bed and breakfast. Oh boy, ✔ breakfast this morning, I'll never forget it. To start with, we had ☐ porridge, then ☐ bacon and ☐ eggs with ☐ sausages, ☐ baked beans and ☐ fried tomatoes. Mrs Campbell made us one of her specialities: ☐ fried bread, just like her children like it. You know, she had baked ✔ bread herself. Of course, there was ☐ orange juice and ☐ tea or ☐ coffee. I actually had ☐ tea, because I didn't like ✔ juice. It was a bit sweet. When we got up from ☐ table, we were so full that we decided not to take ✔ car. We really needed to go for a long walk along ✔ loch. Don't laugh but I took my camera, ✔ new digital one, just in case I saw ☐ Nessie. Unfortunately we didn't, although I had ✔ impression that I saw a funny shape in ✔ mist in ☐ distance. It must be hard for ☐ poor old Nessie. All ✔ tourists that come here want to take ☐ photos of her. Emma, ✔ Campbells' daughter promised to show me the place from where she had once seen ✔ monster.
So much for today,
Florian

## 3 C-test: Hogmanay

Complete the text. Each blank ( ) stands for one letter.

New Year's Eve, 31 De**cember**, is traditionally the most imp**ortant** day in the Highlands, even more important th**an** Christmas. Today people cel**ebrate** with th**eir** friends; they dance, sing, eat and drink. In the past, Hogmanay, the last day of the year, w**as** connected w**ith** a lot of magical rituals[1] to drive out evil powers. So it is no sur**prise** that a lot of dif**ferent** Hogmanay customs ex**isted** all over Scotland. Usually young boys went round the houses, lou**dly** singing "Hogmanay Poems". The boys took p**art** in special rituals called "Hogmanay Lads[2]". They were dre**ssed** in cow skins; one of them cov**ered** with the skin of a bull with the horns and the hooves still on. They made a terrible no**ise** singing and beating the skins and the walls of the ho**uses** with sticks. They were inv**ited** into the houses and offered fo**od** and drink. In some parts of Sc**otland** the man of the house held the skin in the fire and every member of the fa**mily** had to smell the stinking sm**oke** which was beli**eved** to clean the house from anything evil and br**ing** health to the family for the next twelve mo**nths**. The ho**uses** were decorated with holly[3] in order to k**eep** out bad fairies; and juniper[4] was burnt in front of the cattle to pro**tect** them. Cheese was also believed to h**ave** magical powers. A piece of cheese with a h**ole** in it was thought to be esp**ecially** valuable because if a per**son** got lost in the mi**st** in the hills and he lo**oked** through the hole, he w**ould** immediately know where he was.

[1] ['rɪtjuəl] – Ritual, Ritus • [2] [læd] – *Scottish:* boy • [3] ['hɒli] – Stechpalme • [4] ['dʒuːnɪpə] – Wacholder

---

# Unit 3 language B: It makes me so angry!

## 1 Mediation: The test

Iris is furious. She was given a very bad mark for her geography test. Outside the classroom she meets her Scottish exchange partner Liz and her friends. What would their conversation be like in English? Use the following expressions, but don't translate word by word.

> go on about something[1] • to stand • what's it all about? • to mark a test • all over • to be mean • honestly • to join • to enjoy

*Liz:* Was hat dich so wütend gemacht?
*Iris:* Ich hasse sie. Sie hat stundenlang über die Benachteiligten, die Armen, die Blinden und Kranken geredet, über all jene Menschen und Krankheiten in Afrika. Ich kann es nicht mehr ertragen. Irgendwann ist bei jedem einmal die Schmerzgrenze erreicht.
*Liz:* Es ist ja in Ordnung mal Dampf abzulassen. Aber sag mal, worum geht's eigentlich?
*Iris:* Schau her, wie sie meinen Test benotet hat. Die einzige Benachteiligte bin ich. Ich habe so viel gelernt letztes Wochenende. Zwei Stunden lang nach Tinas Geburtstagsparty, bis ich eingeschlafen bin.
*Liz:* Es ist ja überall rot. Und du hast ja nur die Hälfte der Fragen beantwortet.
*Iris:* Sie hat uns nicht genug Zeit gegeben. Sie ist so gemein. Und Julia hat kürzlich mit angehört, wie sie sich über unsere Klasse beschwert hat. Sie wollte sich bloß rächen.
*Liz:* Aber ehrlich, du kannst sie doch nicht verantwortlich machen. Es ist doch nicht ihre Schuld, dass du nach der Party zu müde warst, um zu lernen. Ich hoffe, du warst zu ihr nicht unverschämt. Los, gehen wir zu den andern und machen wir uns einen schönen Nachmittag.

*Liz:* What has made you so angry?
*Iris:* I hate her. She's been going on about the disadvantaged, the poor, the blind and the sick, about all those people and illnesses in Africa. I can't stand it anymore. Everyone has their breaking point, don't they?

_____

*Liz:* It's OK to let off steam, but tell me, what's this all about?

*Iris:* Look, how she (has) marked my test. I'm the only disadvantaged person. I studied so hard last weekend. For two hours after Tina's birthday party until I fell asleep.

*Liz:* It's red all over, and you've only answered half the questions.

*Iris:* She didn't give us enough time. She's so mean. And Julia overheard how she was complaining about our class. She just wanted to take revenge.

*Liz:* But honestly, you can't blame her. It's not her fault that you were too tired to study after the party. I hope you weren't rude to her. Let's join the others and enjoy the afternoon.

[1] stundenlang über etwas reden

## Unit 3 language B

### 2 Vocabulary: Crossword puzzle

**Across →**
1. Ghosts do it.
6. A line of people who are waiting.
7. To divide, to pull things apart.
8. To say it's somebody's fault.
10. A subject or problem that's often discussed.
11. A place for children without parents.
12. An important thing we mustn't waste.

**Down ↓**
2. To believe something is true but not be quite sure.
3. A ... person likes to give things to others.
4. A kind of metal used for making bridges, cars, etc.
5. Some people believe that if you ... a place, bad luck will come to it.
9. A document that allows you to do something.

Across: HAUNT, QUEUE, SEPARATE, BLAME, ISSUE, ORPHANAGE, RESOURCE
Down: ASSUME, GENEROUS, STEEL, CURSE, LICENCE

### 3 Mediation: Singular or plural?

Find the correct translation.

1. Vorsicht! Die Treppe ist sehr steil.
   *Be careful!/Watch out! The stairs are very steep.*

2. Ich kann meine Brille nicht finden. Wo habe ich sie hingelegt?
   *I can't find my glasses. Where did I put them?*

3. Sind die Nachrichten an? – Gut. Schauen wir sie an.
   *Is the news on? – OK. Let's watch it.*

4. Eure neuen Möbel sehen wirklich schön aus. Wo habt ihr sie gekauft?
   *Your new furniture looks really nice. Where did you buy it?*

5. Ich brauche einen Rat.
   *I need a piece of advice.*

6. Die Polizei sucht den Dieb.
   *The police are looking for the thief.*

7. Das Vieh wird bald verkauft werden.
   *The cattle are going to be sold soon.*

8. Die USA sind ein sehr interessantes Land.
   *The USA is a very interesting country.*

### 4 Speaking: At the youth hostel

At the end of their school trip to Stonehaven near Aberdeen Amir's class have to tidy their rooms at the youth hostel. Put in the correct possessive pronouns.

Amir: Is that your sock, Angus?
Angus: No, it isn't ___mine___. Ask Brian, perhaps it's ___his___.
Colin: Hey, Chris, this comic isn't ___yours___, is it? Did Fiona leave it in our room?
Chris: No, it isn't ___mine___ and it isn't ___hers___, either. I gave ___hers___ to Coleen when she looked in this morning. Maybe it's one of Anne's, she has quite a lot of them.

Mr Adams: Amir, Chris, have you got your bags ready?
Amir: Yes, Mr Adams, ___ours___ are packed, but Trevor and Bob haven't finished packing. They can't bring ___theirs___ down yet.
Mr Adams: When all your rooms are tidy, there'll be ice cream for everybody!
Everybody: Great, Mr Adams, that's a fantastic idea of ___yours___.

### 5 Vocabulary: Do or make?

Put in phrases with 'do' or 'make'. Think about the tenses.

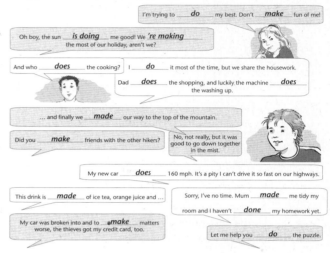

I'm trying to ___do___ my best. Don't ___make___ fun of me!
Oh boy, the sun ___is doing___ me good! We ___'re making___ the most of our holiday, aren't we?
And who ___does___ the cooking? I ___do___ it most of the time, but we share the housework.
Dad ___does___ the shopping, and luckily the machine ___does___ the washing up.
... and finally we ___made___ our way to the top of the mountain.
Did you ___make___ friends with the other hikers? No, not really, but it was good to go down together in the mist.
My new car ___does___ 160 mph. It's a pity I can't drive it so fast on our highways.
This drink is ___made___ of ice tea, orange juice and ...
Sorry, I've no time. Mum ___made___ me tidy my room and I haven't ___done___ my homework yet.
My car was broken into and to ___make___ matters worse, the thieves got my credit card, too.
Let me help you ___do___ the puzzle.

### 6 Reading: A Scotland quiz

Test what you know about Scotland. Use your dictionary for words you don't know. The letters give you the name of a famous Scottish football team:

G L A S G O W   R A N G E R S
1. 2. 3. 4. 5. 6. 7.   8. 9. 10. 11. 12. 13. 14.

1. shortbread
   - B) like a French baguette only shorter
   - ✓ G) a Scottish biscuit
   - E) a short piece of wood used for building bridges in Scotland

2. Highlander
   - O) a special kind of whisky
   - I) a worker on one of the huge oil-rigs
   - ✓ L) a person living in the Scottish mountains

3. Nessie
   - ✓ A) a monster
   - S) Lassie's sister
   - F) a character in a Scottish family series

4. loch
   - V) a cave smugglers use for stolen goods
   - ✓ S) that's what the Scots call their lakes
   - B) a prison in Edinburgh

5. Ben
   - ✓ G) the Scottish word for 'mountain'
   - U) a clock tower in Glasgow
   - R) the Scottish form of 'Benjamin'

6. thistle
   - A) what Scottish boys do when they see a pretty girl
   - ✓ O) (a plant) Scottish symbol on British pound coins
   - F) what Scottish boys call their sisters

7. porridge
   - C) a vegetable with long green leaves
   - ✓ W) what Scots often eat for breakfast
   - T) the shape of the Scottish hills against the sunset

8. haggis
   - A) a Scottish mountain animal with two short legs and two longer ones
   - L) a Scottish square dance
   - ✓ R) a Scottish meat dish

9. lassie
   - ✓ A) Scottish word for a girl
   - H) a Scottish non-alcoholic drink
   - M) a kind of dog from the Highlands

10. hogmanay
    - U) a man who looks after pigs on a Scottish farm
    - P) an animal living in the Highlands
    - ✓ N) the 31st December

11. kilt
    - Q) the past participle of 'to kill'
    - ✓ G) Scottish men wear them sometimes
    - S) a Scottish girl's miniskirt

12. firth
    - U) the title of the Scottish Prime Minister
    - A) the name of a forest tree in Scotland
    - ✓ E) a bay, part of the sea in Scotland

13. tartan
    - ✓ R) the colours and pattern of a Scottish family
    - J) the football shirt worn by Celtic Glasgow
    - F) a Scottish cake

14. Hebrides
    - D) a Scottish boy group
    - ✓ S) a group of islands off the Scottish west coast
    - I) certain stars in Scottish winter skies

## The kiss — Unit 3 text

### 1 Vocabulary: Crossword puzzle

**Across →**
2. A place that is too full of people or things is ...
6. A subject in which you learn how to plan and design buildings.
8. A very wide road on which cars can go fast.
10. You cannot get onto a plane ... you show your boarding pass.
11. If you ... something, you get it from a person that has died and left it to you.
12. A subject or problem that is important and often discussed.

**Down ↓**
1. People use them to light a fire, a candle or a cigarette.
3. If you think that something may not be true, you ... it.
4. All the people who live in a place are its ...
5. People who like to give things to others, e.g. to the poor or to charities, are very ...
6. If you ... something, you think it is true although you do not really know.
7. A traditional kind of food that is eaten for breakfast, e.g. in Scotland and in Scandinavian countries.
9. If something is ..., it is the only one of its kind.

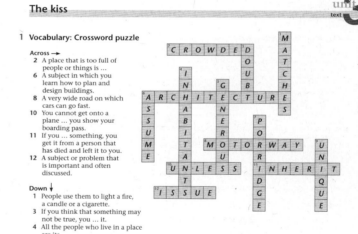

Across: CROWDED, ARCHITECTURE, MOTORWAY, UNLESS, INHERIT, ISSUE
Down: MATCHES, DOUBT, INHABITANTS, GENEROUS, SUPPOSE, PORRIDGE, UNIQUE

### 2 Grammar: Adjectives as nouns

Write down the missing English or German expression.

| English | German |
|---|---|
| the unemployed | die Arbeitslosen |
| a Welsh lady | eine Waliserin |
| some rich people | einige Reiche |
| the rich | die Reichen und |
| and the poor | die Armen |
| a dead man/person | ein Toter |
| three Scotsmen | drei Schotten |
| the English | die Engländer |
| a group of | eine Gruppe von |
| disabled people | Behinderten |
| the little boy | der Kleine |
| the living | die Lebenden |
| and the dead | und die Toten |
| a sick person | ein Kranker |
| a Frenchman | ein Franzose |
| a blind man | ein Blinder |
| the blind | die Blinden |
| a disadvantaged girl | eine Benachteiligte |
| the homeless | die Obdachlosen |
| the needy | die Bedürftigen |
| the good thing about it | das Gute daran |

# unit 3 text

## 3 Vocabulary: Dictionary work

The following expressions all have to do with 'fire'. Look up the words you don't know in your dictionary. Write down the English and German expressions.

1. fire engine — Feuerwehrauto
2. fireman — Feuerwehrmann
3. candles — Kerzen
4. fire extinguisher — Feuerlöscher
5. fire alarm — Feuermelder
6. campfire — Lagerfeuer
7. lighter — Feuerzeug
8. flames — Flammen
9. to light — anzünden
10. fireworks — Feuerwerk
11. to explode — explodieren
12. matches — Steichhölzer

## 4 Listening: A short history of Scottish tartan

Listen to the interview in track 5. Then write complete sentences like those in the listening text using the clues and starting with the words that are given.

1. Mary said that tartan is very popular all over the world.
   Clues: tartan – popular – world

2. The Celts who called themselves Scoti came from Ireland to settle in Scotland in about the 5th century.
   Clues: call themselves – 'Scoti' – come – Ireland – settle – Scotland – 5th century

3. The Scoti used tartan clothes to show their position in the family.
   Clues: use – tartan clothes – show – position – family

4. From the 12th century on, the people in the Lowlands began to learn the language of the north of England.
   Clues: people – Lowlands – begin to learn – language – north of England

5. The climate in Scotland is quite cold and wet, so you need to dress in warm clothes there.
   Clues: cold and wet – need – dress – warm clothes

6. After 1746 only Scottish soldiers and the lowland Scots and women were allowed to wear the tartan.
   Clues: Scottish soldiers – lowland Scots – women – wear – the tartan

## 5 Mixed bag: Error-spotting

Read the sentences about the story 'The kiss'. In one of the four words from each sentence there is a mistake. Mark the wrong word with ✗ and write the correct one on the line below.

1. Chris has always been the odd one out because his face is lopsided and his face has a strange colour and his upper lip is hardly visible.
   odd one | ✗ has | upper | hardly
   is

2. Chris's older sister played with matches when he was three and his cart caught fire with Chris sitting in it.
   Chris's | matches | ✗ cart | sitting
   buggy

3. Mr Conway, their Science teacher, chose Chris for an experience and when he struck a match something caught fire.
   chose | ✗ experience | struck | caught
   experiment

4. Chris admitted that he was only chosen as an assistant for the experiment because he had given a very good mark for his last assignment.
   admitted | had got | ✗ had given | assignment
   had been given

5. Chris's heart was beating fast when Karl held a burning match in front of his face and said he will burn off his eyelashes with it.
   heart | fast | ✗ will | burn off
   would

6. Spike and Karl stopped terrifying Chris with the burning match because Chris said he'd do anything. So Spike meant that they had got a result.
   terrifying | to do | ✗ meant | result
   thought

7. The first few times Chris didn't steel from shops. He took cigarettes from his mum's bag, and a bottle of whisky from the drinks cupboard. Later Chris stole things from Mr Patel's corner shop.
   mum's | ✗ steel | things | Mr Patel's
   steal

8. Chris did not want to appear a coward in front of Shelby. And although he felt like a wimp he wanted Shelby to admire him. But when he saw that Karl had inspired the fireworks …
   coward | wimp | admire | ✗ inspired
   lit

9. Chris noticed that Shelby's eyes were wide of horror and he thought that it was because his face was so close to hers. Shelby shouted, pushed Chris to one side and reached for the firework.
   noticed | ✗ wide of | close to | reached for
   wide with

## 6 Listening: Museums in Edinburgh

a) Listen to track 6. Mr Stuart talks about seven museums. Can you match their names with what you can see in them? b) Listen again to check your answers.

- The Museum of Scotland — The history of the Scottish people
- The Museum of Scottish Life — Farm animals
- The Concorde Museum — The fastest passenger plane
- The Royal Museum — Art objects
- Museum of Costume — Clothes
- Interactive Science and Technology Gallery — Science and space travel
- The Museum of Childhood — Children's toys and games

---

# unit 3 let's check — Young people in Scotland

## 1 Mediation: In English, please

1. Können Sie mir bitte Feuer geben? — Can you give me a light, please?
2. Machen wir doch ein Lagerfeuer! — Let's make a campfire./Why don't we make a campfire.
3. Wer hat den Feueralarm ausgelöst? — Who has set off the fire alarm?
4. Sein Onkel ist schon seit 20 Jahren Feuerwehrmann. — His uncle has been a fireman/firefighter for 20 years.
5. Bei den Thomsons brennt ein Feuer (im Kamin). — The Thomsons have a fire going.
6. Sie schafften es nicht den Waldbrand zu löschen. — They didn't manage to put out/to extinguish the forest fire.
7. Hast du schon einmal ein richtiges Feuerwerk gesehen? — Have you ever seen a proper firework display/proper fireworks?
8. Sei vorsichtig, dass deine Bluse nicht Feuer fängt! — Be careful/Watch out that your blouse doesn't catch fire.
9. Irgendjemand hat den Schuppen unserer Nachbarn in Brand gesteckt. — Somebody has set our neighbours' shed on fire./Somebody has set fire to our neighbours' shed.

## 2 Grammar: Singular and plural words

Fill in the correct English expressions.

1. For **more/further information** (weitere Auskünfte) please apply to the manager.
2. He gave me several **pieces of good advice** (gute Ratschläge) on how to repair my computer, but the best **advice was** (Ratschlag • war) to buy a new one.
3. Could you lend me **your jeans** (deine Jeans), please? – No, I'm sorry, I want to wear **them** (sie) myself. Why don't you wear your own **trousers/pants** (Hose)?
4. A lot of people think **Math(ematic)s is** (Mathematik • ist) a very difficult subject.
5. Look, my mother has bought **some/a pair of sunglasses** (eine Sonnenbrille) for our holiday.
6. "No news **is** (to be) good news," Grandpa Jones used to say when he didn't get any mail.
7. Oh, Gary, just look at **this furniture** (diese Möbel)! **Isn't it** (Sind sie nicht) wonderful? – Yes, of course, but 3,000 pounds **is** (to be) a lot of money!

---

# Focus on the New World — focus 2

## 1 Vocabulary: The alphabet competition

You can play the alphabet game with a friend as it is described on page 142 in your text book. Here is another version. Fill in the words defined on the right.

| | | |
|---|---|---|
| a | as best we can | If we try to do something very, very well, we do it … |
| b | board | a nicely cut flat piece of wood (You can build a cabin with it.) |
| c | coin | hard, round pieces of money → |
| d | disease | another word for illness |
| e | effect | a change or event that is the result of something |
| f | freak | a person that is strange, because of his or her looks or opinions |
| g | guide dog | an animal that is trained to help blind people to find their way |
| h | hurry | People who do not have enough time are in a … |
| i | independence | complete freedom from others → |
| j | Japanese | the people who live in Japan |
| k | knight | a brave and noble person of the Middle Ages |
| l | laugh | you do this when you hear a good joke |
| m | medical | adjective of 'medicine' |
| n | nod | to say 'yes' by moving your head up and down |
| o | permanent | something that lasts for a very long time or forever |
| p | Puritans | religious group of the 17th century → |
| q | Quakers | They settled in Pennsylvania. → |
| r | religion | noun of 'religious' |
| s | storehouse | a building used to keep goods in |
| t | trade | to exchange, buy or sell goods |
| u | ugly | opposite of 'beautiful' |
| v | vicar | A priest is to a Catholic what a … is to a Protestant. |
| w | wooden | made from wood |
| x | Xmas | a shorter way of writing 'Christmas' in English |
| y | yummy | you say this when something tastes delicious |
| z | zippers | Some clothes do not have buttons, they have … |

# Unit 4 intro: New England

## 1 Reading: The Pilgrims as people

In each line one word is missing. Complete the text – as shown in line 1 – with the words in the box.

through • difficulties • themselves • country • familiar • shared • surrounded • heroes • emigrating • in • example • the • were • escape • communities • without • who • of

### The Pilgrims as people: Understanding the Plymouth colonists

The people we know as the Pilgrims have become with so many legends **surrounded**
that we almost forget that they were real people. In spite of great they **difficulties**
bravely made the famous 1620 voyage[1] and founded first New England **the**
colony, but they were still ordinary English men and women, not super **heroes**
If we really want to understand them, we must try to look behind the
legends and see them as they saw **themselves**
They were English people who wanted to the religious controversies[2] and **escape**
economic problems of their time by to America. Many of the Pilgrims **emigrating**
were Puritans. They believed that membership in the Church England was **of**
against the rules in the bible, and that they had to break away and form
independent Christian which were truer to God. At a time when Church **communities**
and State one, such an act was against the law and the Puritans had to leave **were**
their mother **country**
As English people, the Pilgrims also a living culture. They were not people **shared**
just like ourselves but dressed in funny clothes, or a primitive folk our **without**
technology, but a strong and courageous[3] people embodied the best **who**
elements of their exciting society. They brought their own culture to the
New World and tried to set a good of English society on the edge of an alien **example**
continent. They were not pioneers making a trail the wilderness to the **through**
future. They were English men and women with their customs, doing their **familiar**
best to continue[4] the lives they knew back home spite of the unfamiliar **in**
surroundings.

[1] [vɔɪdʒ] – Schiffsreise • [2] [ˈkɒntrəvɜːsi] – Auseinandersetzung • [3] [kəˈreɪdʒəs] – mutig • [4] [kənˈtɪnjuː] – weitermachen

---

# Unit 4 language A: An e-mail from Susie

## 1 Vocabulary: Opposites

wealthy ↔ **poor**
**full/crowded** ↔ empty
interior ↔ **exterior**
**hardware** ↔ software
to get married ↔ **to get divorced**
**independent** ↔ dependent
unspectacular ↔ **spectacular**

to decrease ↔ **to increase**
relaxation ↔ tension
advantage ↔ **disadvantage**
coward ↔ hero
beautiful ↔ **ugly**
**disease/illness** ↔ health
boring ↔ **interesting**

## 2 Writing: Explaining words

Explain the **marked** words with a complete sentence. Use one expression from the box in each sentence.

*may be • might be • perhaps • probably • certainly • possibly • most likely*

1. a **useless** tin opener (wahrscheinlich)

1. That probably is a tin opener that is of not much use or that simply doesn't work.

2. an **enjoyable** evening (kann sein)
2. This may be an evening when you have a lot of fun or when you simply enjoy yourself.

3. an **inexperienced** leader (vielleicht)
3. That is a leader who hasn't got much experience in what he's doing, perhaps because he's new in his job.

4. a **spectacular** video clip (könnte sein)

4. This might be a video clip that is rather unusual or that attracts the viewers' attention in some other way.

5. an **unforgettable** journey (höchstwahrscheinlich)
5. This is most likely a trip that you'll want to remember for ever, because it was so nice.

6. an **eventful** summer holiday (sicherlich)
6. That certainly is a holiday when a lot of things happened.

7. an **unsinkable** ferry (möglicherweise)

7. This is possibly a ferry that has been built or constructed so that it won't/can't sink.

---

# Unit 4 language A

## 3 Speaking: Bits of conversations

Complete what these people say – with suitable gerunds and prepositions. Use these verbs:

do • spend • live • travel • speak • wait • learn • hike • jog

1. Are you looking forward **to spending** your holiday in the south of France?
2. Barbara loves all sports apart **from jogging**.
3. My brother is interested **in learning** to ride a motor-bike. Can you teach him?
4. Have you ever thought **of hiking** in the mountains for a few days? It's good exercise.
5. Sorry, I'm not used **to doing** such hard work. I'm only a student after all.
6. What **about waiting** for the next bus? It's much cheaper than taking a taxi.
7. Most young Europeans are keen **on travelling** to other countries even if they are not so good **at speaking** the language.
8. Has your sister got used **to living** so far away from home or is she still homesick[1]?

[1] [ˈhəʊmsɪk] – Heimweh haben

---

# Unit 4 language B: The 1627 Pilgrim Village

## 1 Speaking: Going on vacation in New England

Sarah and Gary Higgins were talking about their next holiday. Write down what they said and decide whether to use a gerund (plus preposition) or an infinitive.

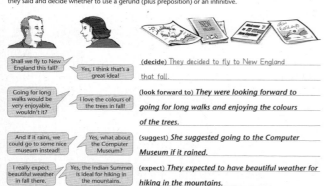

- Shall we fly to New England this fall? / Yes, I think that's a great idea!
  (decide) They decided to fly to New England that fall.
- Going for long walks would be very enjoyable, wouldn't it? / I love the colours of the trees in fall!
  (look forward to) They were looking forward to going for long walks and enjoying the colours of the trees.
- And if it rains, we could go to some nice museum instead! / Yes, what about the Computer Museum?
  (suggest) She suggested going to the Computer Museum if it rained.
- I really expect beautiful weather in fall there. / Yes, the Indian Summer is ideal for hiking in the mountains.
  (expect) They expected to have beautiful weather for hiking in the mountains.

---

# Unit 4 language B

- Where should we stay then? / Hotels are rather expensive in that area, aren't they?
  (complain) She complained about hotels being rather expensive in that area.
- Maybe we could stay on one of those farms in Vermont. / Yes, with a wonderful view of the rolling hills.
  (think) He thought of/about staying on one of those beautiful farms in Vermont.
- Do you think we could also go to Cape Cod? / I'm not quite sure if we'll have time enough to do that.
  (not know) They didn't know whether to go to Cape Cod./if they would have enough time to go to Cape Cod.
- It's so difficult to book a room on the Internet. / Why don't you just give them a call, Gary?
  (want) She wanted her husband to give them a call.
- We could have some lobster in some fishing port on the coast. / But they are terribly expensive even there!
  (be worth) She thought it wasn't worth having any lobster in one of those fishing ports.

## 2 Mediation: A teacher's thoughts after a visit to the Pilgrim Village

Say it in English by using gerund constructions.

1. Es hat sich wirklich gelohnt, die Plymouth Colony mit meinen Schülern zu besuchen.
It was really worth **visiting Plymouth Colony with my students.**

2. Sie waren sehr daran interessiert, das Leben der frühen Siedler kennen zu lernen.
**They were very interested in getting to know about the life of the early settlers.**

3. Nur einer von ihnen beschwerte sich darüber, dass er keine Gelegenheit hatte, sich mit einem der Rollenspieler zu unterhalten.
**Only one of them complained about having no opportunity to talk to one of the role players.**

4. Allerdings mochten einige die Vorstellung nicht, über ihren Ausflug ein Referat halten zu müssen.
**However, a few/some of them didn't like the idea/thought of having to give a talk/report/presentation on their trip/excursion.**

5. Was haltet ihr davon, zu versuchen in der Plymouth Colony einen Ferienjob zu bekommen?
**What about trying to get/What do you think of getting a holiday job at Plymouth Colony?**

# Unit 4 language B

## 3 Writing: The Thompsons at Hobbamock's Homesite

Connect the sentences by using gerunds together with the words on the right.

*instead of • without • in spite of • apart from • by*

1. When the Thompsons wanted to go into the museum shop, it was too crowded with people. So they went to Hobbamock's Homesite.

   Instead of going into the crowded museum shop, the Thompsons went to Hobbamock's Homesite.

2. Although they visited Hobbamock's Homesite, they didn't have a chance to talk to one of the Native Americans there.

   In spite of visiting Hobbamock's Homesite, they didn't have a chance to talk to one of the Native Americans there.

3. The Thompsons did just about everything during their stay there, but they didn't taste any of the food made by the Native Americans.

   Apart from tasting some of the food made by the Native Americans, the Thompsons did just about everything during their stay there.

4. In the end they learned a lot about the history of the early settlers. They read an excellent guide book about them.

   In the end they learned a lot about the history of the early settlers by reading an excellent guide book about them.

## 4 Grammar: Infinitive or gerund?

**W i n t h r o p**
1 2 3 4 5 6 7 8

Draw a circle around the letter next to the correct verb forms and write the letters in the boxes above. If your answers are right, you'll get the name of one of the Pilgrims' religious leaders. His name was John …

1. David has been looking forward (visit) the Pilgrim Village with his classmates all week.
   **(w)** to visiting   x to visit   y visiting

2. He simply couldn't imagine (cross) the Atlantic in a sailing ship like that?
   g to cross   h at crossing   **(i)** crossing

3. Nobody stopped (talk). It was impossible for their teacher (hear) the guide's explanations.
   **(l)** to talk – to hear   m in order to talk – to hear   o talking – to hear

4. "What do you think (have) a break before (go) to Hobbamock's Homesite?" Mr Hooker asked.
   r having – going   s about having – to go   **(t)** of having – going

5. "Are you keen (eat) some of their food? Or would you prefer (have) your sandwiches?"
   g on eating – having   **(h)** on eating – to have   i to eat – to have

6. Some of the role players find it hard to get used (speak) this 17th century English dialect.
   **(r)** to speaking   s to speak   t speaking

7. It was fascinating (watch) the women at work. They were so clever (handle) the enormous pots.
   m to watch – to handle   n watching – handling   **(o)** to watch – at handling

8. In spite (have) to walk a lot, most of the students thought it was really worth (come) here.
   **(p)** of having – coming   q to have – to come   r of having – to come

---

# The ransom — text

## 1 Vocabulary: Word families

| noun | adjective | noun | adjective |
|---|---|---|---|
| *importance* | important | *value* | valuable |
| wood | **wooden** | poison | **poisonous** |
| *independence* | independent | *fascination* | fascinating |
| fury | **furious** | enjoyment | **enjoyable** |
| *depression* | depressed | *electricity* | electric |
| religion | **religious** | generosity | **generous** |
| *specialty* | special | *spectacle* | spectacular |
| divorce | **divorced** | medicine | **medical** |

Now use suitable nouns or adjectives from the lists to complete these sentences.

1. Did you hear that a __valuable__ painting has been stolen from the National Gallery?
2. When the USA became __independent__ in 1776, the British started a war against them.
3. In the past people used __wooden__ spoons and forks, because metal was expensive.
4. Everybody knows about the __importance__ of London as the capital of Britain.
5. Sometimes a __divorce__ is the only answer to the problems of married couples.
6. The Baxters like giving money to the poor. They are well-known for their __generosity__.
7. The __enjoyment__ Mr Gregg gets out of playing golf is unbelievable. He simply loves it.

## 2 Mediation: Prepositions

Express these phrases in English but think about the prepositions.

1. Ab / Auf nach Massachusetts! — **1. Off to Massachusetts!**
2. Gehen wir doch in die Innenstadt! — **2. Let's go downtown./Let's go to the city centre.**
3. Da ist ein Flugzeug am Himmel. — **3. There's a plane in the sky.**
4. Er ist gut im Kochen, aber schlecht im Feuer machen. — **4. He's good at cooking, but bad at making a fire.**
5. Das ist eine CD von den Red Hot Chili Peppers. — **5. That's a CD by the Red Hot Chili Peppers.**
6. Lassen Sie mich bitte hier aussteigen! — **6. Let me get off/out here, please!**
7. Die Pilger übergaben ein wichtiges Dokument. — **7. The Pilgrims handed over an important document.**

---

# Unit 4 text

8. Cambridge liegt direkt neben Boston. — **8. Cambridge is right next to Boston.**
9. Susie kann heute nicht in die Schule gehen. — **9. Susie can't go to school today.**
10. Das hat er absichtlich gemacht! — **10. He did that on purpose.**
11. Warum ist er auf der Flucht? — **11. Why is he on the run?**
12. Können Sie das Ergebnis der Ermittlungen zusammenfassen? — **12. Can you sum up the result of the inquiry?**
13. Kate ist gern unterwegs. — **13. Kate likes being out and about.**
14. Meiner Meinung nach ist der Herbst die beste Jahreszeit zum Wandern. — **14. In my opinion fall is the best season for hiking.**
15. Du hältst die Landkarte falsch herum. — **15. You are holding the map the wrong way round/upside down.**
16. Er ist krank vor Angst. — **16. He's sick with fear.**
17. Ihre Augen waren vor Entsetzen weit (aufgerissen). — **17. Her eyes were wide with horror.**

## 3 Vocabulary: Find the missing words

*let off steam • Frenchman • homeless • lovesick • useless • get off • seasick*
*hopeless • Dutchman • fall off • homesick • Englishman*

1. Romeo and Juliet were __lovesick__.
2. On a boat in strong wind you may get __seasick__.
3. Far away from friends and family you might get __homesick__.
4. When you are very angry, you might want to __let off steam__.
5. Without a helmet you might get hurt when you __fall off__ your bike.
6. You can __get off__ the bus at any stop you like.
7. A __Frenchman__ usually likes wine and cheese.
8. A true __Englishman__ will probably drink his tea with milk.
9. A __Dutchman__ is someone who comes from the Netherlands.
10. People who have no place to live are __homeless__.
11. If you have nothing to look forward to, your situation is rather __hopeless__.
12. Something that is good for nothing is __useless__.

---

## 4 Writing: Paraphrasing

Explain what the **marked** expressions mean by paraphrasing them.

1. Many people watched the fight, but nobody wanted to get **involved**.
   **1. Many people watched the fight, but nobody felt like doing anything about it./…, but nobody wanted to step in.**

2. It really was a big **feast** when John and Diana got married.
   **2. When John and Diana got married, they had a large and very special meal.**

3. He **enclosed** a 20 dollar bill in his letter.
   **3. He put the bill in with the letter.**

4. They couldn't **provide** us with **appropriate** shoes before we started our mountain tour.
   **4. They were not able to give us the kind of shoes we needed for that tour.**

5. Do you have any **coins** on you? I'd like to buy a newspaper.
   **5. Money, but no paper money or bills. Just some small change. Hard, round pieces of money.**

6. Did you hear that my younger brother has got **engaged** to a girl from his college?
   **6. They are planning to get married, but they aren't married yet.**

7. They **obviously** made a mistake when they packed the keyboard for my computer.
   **7. It's easy to see that they made a mistake when they packed the keyboard for the computer.**

## 5 Vocabulary: Crossword puzzle

**Down ↓**
1. Chairs, tables, cupboards, etc.
2. Something that is easy to see or to understand is …
3. Wood that is used for building.
4. To give someone the idea for something (e.g. a poem, a song).
5. A plan that you make for the future, usually with somebody else.
8. Noun of 'angry'.

**Across →**
6. The person who tells a story.
7. The world or area we live in; everything around us.
9. Another word for 'police officer'.
10. A line of people who are waiting, e.g. at a bus stop or at the supermarket.
11. You type on it when you use your computer.

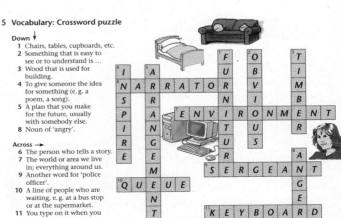

Crossword answers shown: NARRATOR, ENVIRONMENT, SERGEANT, QUEUE, KEYBOARD (with down entries: FURNITURE, OBVIOUS, TIMBER, INSPIRE, ARRANGEMENT, RAGE).

# Unit 4

## 6 Listening: An interesting job

Listen to track 7 and put the parts of the story about Mr Fox's watch in the right order.

4  1. Mr Fox tells the pupils to write an essay.
8  2. Mr Fox puts the book on the table.
6  3. A girl draws a cartoon of Mr Fox on the board.
10 4. Mr Fox looks surprised.
3  5. Mr Fox asks the pupils if they have seen the watch.
5  6. Mr Fox leaves the classroom.
1  7. Mr Fox enters the classroom looking worried.
9  8. Mr Fox lifts the book up and finds the watch.
7  9. Mr Fox comes back into the classroom carrying a book.
2  10. Mr Fox says his watch has been stolen.

## 7 Listening: A short history of the Mayflower

a) Before listening to track 8 make sure you know what these two words mean. Then listen to the text.

**voyage:** a journey often by sea
**anniversary:** a day on which something special or historical is remembered; it's a bit like a birthday

b) Decide if these 20 statements are true, false or not in the text. Listen again and check your answers.

|    | Statement | true | false | not in the text |
|---|---|---|---|---|
| 1. | In 1620, a ship called the *Mayflower* sailed to America. | ✓ | | |
| 2. | The *Mayflower* was very big. | | ✓ | |
| 3. | The *Speedwell* was painted blue and white. | | | ✓ |
| 4. | The *Mayflower* was 11 years old in 1620. | | ✓ | |
| 5. | John Carver was French. | | ✓ | |
| 6. | Only men travelled to America. | | | ✓ |
| 7. | The *Mayflower* sailed from Southampton on August 15th. | ✓ | | |
| 8. | They turned back twice because too much water was coming into the *Mayflower*. | | ✓ | |
| 9. | The *Speedwell* was carrying 102 passengers. | | ✓ | |
| 10. | The voyage took 65 days. | | ✓ | |
| 11. | The *Mayflower* arrived in America on November 5th. | | ✓ | |
| 12. | 41 men agreed on the *Mayflower* Compact. | | ✓ | |
| 13. | John Carver was not the first leader. | | ✓ | |
| 14. | Plymouth in America was named after Plymouth in England. | ✓ | | |
| 15. | The *Mayflower*'s passengers did not have enough food on the ship. | | | ✓ |
| 16. | The winter of 1620–1621 was terrible. | ✓ | | |
| 17. | The *Mayflower* arrived back in England on June 16th. | | ✓ | |
| 18. | In 1957, a ship called the *Mayflower II* was built by America as a present to England. | | ✓ | |
| 19. | The *Mayflower II* had no engine. | ✓ | | |
| 20. | The *Mayflower II* is now in Plymouth, Massachusetts. | ✓ | | |

---

# New England — let's check

## 1 Grammar: Gerunds and infinitives

Fill in the correct verb forms, add prepositions and make other necessary changes.

1. Some boys in our class **were crazy about smoking** (crazy • smoke) until our teacher showed us photos of **what smoking** (smoke) can do to your lungs. /3 /2
2. **Are you looking forward to inviting** (you • look forward • invite) all your friends to the party on Saturday? /3
3. Are you keen **on swimming** (swim)? Or would **you prefer to go** (you • prefer • go) for a walk along the beach? /2 /1
4. Mr and Mrs Smith **have been dreaming of having** (dream • have) their own house ever since they got married. In the end they **decided to build** (decide • build) one themselves. /3 /2
5. My girlfriend **wants to be** (want • be) a singer in our rock band, but I think she is **really bad at singing** (real • bad • sing). /2 /3
6. When I was still at university, I couldn't **imagine doing** (imagine • do) a regular job, which also **meant getting up** (mean • get up) early. /1 /2
7. "What **about spending** (spend) a few days at the seaside in a nice little fishing port? Would you **be interested in doing** (interested • do) that? /2 /2
8. In a big city like Boston, Mike **simply cannot get used to living** (simple • cannot • get used • live) in an apartment all by himself. /4
9. We suggested **going hiking** (go • hike) in the mountains, but Susan was so worried **about driving** (drive) on icy roads that we **decided not to do** (decide • not • do) it in the end. /2 /2 /2
10. Bill never complained **about having to work** (have • work) long hours. And he **didn't worry about being paid** (not • worry • be paid) enough because he simply liked **doing** (do) his job. He never **expected to be fired** (expect • be fired) without warning. /2 /3 /1 /2
11. My uncle prefers **driving** (drive) to **being driven** (be driven). But he can't stand **sitting** (sit) behind the steering wheel for too long. /2 /2 /1
12. **Do you want me to check** (want • me • check) the solutions for you now? /2

Now check your solutions and see how many points you've got: /50

---

## 2 Mediation: Role player at the Pilgrim Village

Say it in English by using infinitive constructions.

1. Ich möchte, dass die Leute erkennen, dass das Leben im 17. Jahrhundert nicht so einfach war.
   **I want people to realize that life in the 17th century wasn't that easy.**
2. Es war fast unmöglich für die Siedler, den ersten Winter zu überleben.
   **It was almost impossible for the settlers to survive the first winter.**
3. Die Pilgerväter waren nicht die Einzigen, die nach Amerika auswanderten.
   **The Pilgrims weren't the only ones to emigrate to America.**
4. Und sie waren nicht die Letzten, die aus religiösen Gründen über den Atlantik hierher kamen.
   **And they weren't the last to come here across the Atlantic for religious reasons.**

## 3 Grammar: Moving to Baltimore

Fill in the correct verb form.

1. stay  follow  know  must move  be

I **have known** Tom Taylor **for** (seit) more than five years now. Unfortunately his father **had to move** to Baltimore two months ago. Tom and his mother **are going to follow** him next spring. If Tom **stayed** here in Boston, I **would be** much happier.

2. not worry  feel  sit  like  give  tell

Look, there's Tom's grandmother. She **has been sitting** by the window all afternoon. — I wonder how she **'ll like** it when she's taken to the old people's home next month. — Only yesterday Tom said he **felt** sorry he **had given** her so much trouble recently, but his mother **told** him **not to worry** so much.

3. hear  go  be  sleep  talk  not hear

A few days ago his grandmother **was sleeping** in her armchair when Tom and I **went** into the room, so she **didn't hear** what we **were talking** about. If she **had been** awake, she **would have heard** how much Tom worries about her.

4. spend  finish  celebrate  build

The Taylors' new house **is being built** at the moment, and Mr Taylor hopes it **'ll be finished** by the end of next month, so that they can **spend** their Christmas holidays together. They **'re going to celebrate** New Year's Eve with their friends.

---

# Units 3+4 revision

## 1 Grammar: Travelling is fun!?

Fill in the correct verb form, add 'since' or 'for' and missing prepositions.

Mr and Mrs Barnett **have known** (know) each other **for** more than 30 years. They both like **getting to know** (get to know) other countries. They **have made** (make) trips to almost every country in Europe **since** they **met** (meet) for the first time **at** college. Mr Barnett **has been** (be) a businessman **since** he **finished** (finish) college in 1983. He likes **flying** (fly) a lot and he **flies** (fly) to the USA **on** business regularly.

Last month, the Barnetts **travelled** (travel) **to** Paris together. Before that, they **had been learning** (learn) French **for** at least six months. And they **had been taught** (teach) a lot of useful expressions by Monsieur Dubois, their French neighbour. Mrs Barnett enjoys **travelling** (travel) with her husband. Sometimes she wonders if they **'ll ever go** (ever • go) to Turkey together, because she'd like to see Istanbul so much. But today it's Rome. They **'ve been waiting** (wait) for their flight **since** eight in the morning and they **'ve just been told** (just • tell) by an airline official that their plane **is still being serviced** (still • service). **Travelling** (travel) abroad is not always fun after all!

†[sː:vɪs] – warten, technisch überprüfen

## 2 Mixed bag: Error-spotting

Underline the mistake and write the correct word on the right. There is one mistake in each sentence.

1. It's top secret, but she'll tell you <u>when</u> you promise not to inform her boss. — **if**
2. If Harry <u>would have</u> a new car, he would show it to everybody, I'm sure. — **had**
3. If Christopher doesn't arrive soon, we <u>start</u> watching the DVD without him. — **will start**
4. If you <u>will fly</u> to Chicago with Lufthansa before 15th of June, it will cost you only 350 euros. — **fly**
5. You can't enter this building <u>when</u> you do not show your identity card. — **if you do not show/unless you show**
6. If I had known that there was plenty of time, I <u>hadn't taken</u> a taxi to get here. — **wouldn't have taken**
7. Margret wouldn't have asked you for help if she <u>would have known</u> how to do it herself. — **had known**
8. My brother would tell you how to design your own homepage if he <u>would know</u> how to do it. — **knew**
9. <u>If</u> you arrive in London, I'll meet you at Heathrow Airport. Don't worry, I won't be late. — **When**

# Unit 5 — Fame and fortune

## 1 Vocabulary: Crossword puzzle

1 Only.
2 He really likes being a teacher, teaching is his …
3 Flats in London are very expensive. They cost a …
4 Noun of 'famous'.
5 If you … something, you think it is really good.
6 Pupils who have a positive … to school, usually get better marks.
7 The negative side of something, e.g. a job.
8 If you … yourself to something, you spend a lot of time on it.
9 If you cannot imagine something happening, it's … your wildest dreams.
10 Real.
11 To try hard.

Crossword answers:
1 MERELY
2 CALLING
3 FORTUNE
4 FAME
5 APPRECIATE
6 ATTITUDE
7 DISADVANTAGE
8 COMMIT
9 BEYOND
10 AUTHENTIC
11 STRIVE

## 2 Grammar: Pop stars

Complete the sentences in a) with suitable words. Then rewrite the sentences to say what would be/might be/would have been, if things were/had been different.

1. a) Will Smith is so **successful** because he works hard.
   b) If he **didn't work so hard, he wouldn't be so successful.**

2. a) Avril Lavigne was in the right place at the right time when she was **discovered**.
   b) If she **hadn't been in the right place at the right time, she might not have been discovered.**

3. a) Orlando Bloom enjoys **being** an actor very much because he likes **dressing** up and becoming somebody else.
   b) If he **didn't like dressing up and becoming somebody else, he wouldn't enjoy being an actor.**

4. a) Robbie Williams **left** his former band *Take That* in 1997, so today he is one of the world's top solo musicians.
   b) If Robbie **hadn't left his former band** *Take That* **in 1997, he wouldn't be one of the world's top solo musicians today.**

---

# The audition

## 1 Grammar: Adverbs

Choose one of the following adverbs and complete the sentences. Use each adverb only once.

usually • actually • unfortunately • generally • apparently • in fact • frankly • obviously • hopefully

1. The audience did not clap their hands – they **obviously** hadn't liked Mike's performance!
2. **Unfortunately** Mike had a cold, so his voice sounded strange.
3. **Frankly**, his performance was a disaster!
4. **Hopefully** the next singer will be better!
5. **Usually** the audiences at shows like "Pop Idol"[1] go crazy.
6. **Sometimes** they actually throw things onto the stage.
7. **In fact** that happens quite often.
8. But **generally** they behave well.
9. **Apparently** the next boy, who has just started singing, is better – great!

[1] British version of *Deutschland sucht den Superstar*

## 2 Cloze test: The contest[1]

Complete the text.

Many of the young people who **have taken** part in contests like "Pop Idol" **have** never been heard of again. Although **millions** of people watched them on TV, **hardly** anybody remembers their names today. Even **if** they had one or two hit **singles** in the charts, they did not **make** a fortune with them, as **especially** young people like to think. Once they **had** spent all their money, most of **them** went back to what they had **been** doing before they became famous for a couple of weeks. Others tried hard **to** stay in the spotlight[2] for a **little/bit** longer – even if it was by **causing** scandals or moving into a container **for** a while in order to be **filmed** 24 hours a day. But even **those** of their former fans who had **admired** them most were soon no longer **interested** in them. Some got the chance **to** record a complete album, but only **very** few of them have really become **successful** artists. Some others got into trouble **with** the police, and a few even **tried** to kill themselves – or actually did!

[1] ['kɔntest] – Wettbewerb • [2] ['spɒtlaɪt] – Rampenlicht

---

## 3 Writing: The pool

Make sentences. Think about the word order and the verb forms.

1. pool • Clyde • summer • often • the • to • go • in
   **(In summer) Clyde often goes to the pool (in summer).**

2. not like • much • obviously • very • swimming • he • but
   **But (obviously) he (obviously) doesn't like swimming very much.**

3. never • the • we • water • in fact • see • in • him • actually
   **In fact we have never actually seen him in the water.**

4. not be • swim • particularly • on • I • keen • actually
   **Actually I'm not particularly keen on swimming.**

5. I • hot • usually • days • into • really • on • jump • pool • the • for a minute • but
   **But (on really hot days) I usually jump into the water for a minute (on really hot days).**

6. Clyde • be • apparently • water • or • afraid • swim • not can • of • perhaps • but • he
   **But apparently Clyde is afraid of water – or perhaps he can't swim.**

## 4 Mediation / Writing: Meet your favourite pop star!

Imagine you have won tickets for a concert by your favourite pop star. After the concert you will even have the chance to talk to him. He doesn't speak German, so you have to think of questions you would like to ask him in English. Write down the questions you and your friends have collected.

Wir wollen wissen, …
1. … wie er es geschafft hat, so erfolgreich zu sein.
2. … ob er oft zum Vorsingen mit anderen jugendlichen Teilnehmern (= *Künstlern*) gehen musste.
3. … ob seine Eltern ihn dazu ermutigt haben, Popstar zu werden.
4. … ob er ein sehr ehrgeiziger Mensch ist.
5. … ob es ihm nichts ausmacht, so viel Zeit in Hotels zu verbringen.
6. … ob er sich bei einem seiner Konzerte jemals in ein Mädchen aus dem Publikum verliebt hat.

1. **How did you manage to be so successful?**
2. **Did you often have to go to auditions with other teenage performers?**
3. **Did your parents encourage you to become a pop star?**
4. **Are you a very ambitious person?**
5. **Don't you mind spending so much time in hotels?**
6. **Have you ever fallen in love with a girl from the audience at one of your concerts?**

---

# After the audition

## 1 Speaking: Formal and informal English

a) Decide which sentences are formal and which are informal English.
b) Underline the words or phrases that tell you and give a short explanation on the right. The words and phrases in the tip on the right may help you.
c) Find the pairs that belong together and number them like this: f1, f2 etc. (= formal) i1, i2 etc. (= informal).

**tip**
formal: subclauses, passive voice, exact, long forms, words of Latin / French origin, formal vocabulary;
informal: simple sentences, active voice; exaggeration; short forms simple / colloquial vocabulary

| Sentence | No. | Explanation |
|---|---|---|
| We were kept waiting for nearly 45 minutes. | f1 | passive voice, exact |
| I wish to apologize for being so rude to you. | f2 | formal vocabulary, word of French origin |
| As I was having a really interesting conversation with a young man I had met at the airport, I wasn't keen on boarding the plane. | f3 | long sentence, subclause |
| They left us sitting there for hours. | i1 | exaggeration, colloquial |
| We spend considerable sums of money on eating out. | f4 | word of Latin origin, formal vocabulary |
| Her house is in the middle of nowhere. | i5 | exaggeration |
| She lives in a village that is located about 20 km away from the nearest town. | f5 | exact |
| I had a chat with that guy out there. Didn't feel like hopping on the plane. | i3 | colloquial vocabulary |
| Sorry, I shouldn't have called you names. | i2 | short form, simple vocabulary |
| We fork out tons of money on food and drink in pubs. | i4 | colloquial vocabulary |

## 2 Mixed bag: Error-spotting

Find the mistake in each line, underline the wrong word and write down the correct one on the right.

After the audition Mrs Simons told Mrs Denker <u>at</u> the phone what had — **on**
happened. She complained about the way in which the <u>hole</u> event had — **whole**
been organised, and <u>particular</u> about the fact that they had been kept — **particularly**
waiting for a <u>condiserable</u> time before the director arrived. Another — **considerable**
thing she had not appreciated was the <u>unnecessary</u> large number of — **unnecessarily**
hopeful young performers who <u>had invited</u> to the audition. When Mrs — **had been invited**
Denker asked if Billy had received a <u>backcall</u> yet, that made her even — **callback**
more angry, and she promised <u>writing</u> a letter. — **to write**

## 3 Writing: A letter of complaint

**a)** Dave from London went on a coach trip to watch a football match in Hamburg. Read what he told his friend Alan on the phone after he had come back home.

Hi Alan, It's me, Dave! I've just come back from Hamburg. (…) What it was like? It was hell! (…) Well, let me start with the drive to Hamburg. You know how long it took us to get to the ferry? Four hours! (…) Well, we had to pick up quite a few people, and some of them in the middle of nowhere, too! So we missed our ferry and had to wait for the next one – so no more sightseeing in Hamburg. The next shock came when I found out that I didn't have a single room. There was another man in my room! (…) Then I had to take the underground to the stadium, because the coach had disappeared. (…) Of course I got there more than half an hour late, but what was even worse was my seat! It was right behind one of the goals! (…) At night I could not sleep because of all the cars going past! (…) The breakfast in the morning was a joke – just coffee and toast! (…) And then all that way back home again! What a trip! (…) You can be sure of that, I'll write them a letter immediately! They have to give me some of my money back! See you tomorrow, Alan. Bye!

**b)** Complete Dave's formal letter of complaint to the coach company.

The Football Coach
21 Upper Street
London

42 Queens Drive
London
5th March

Dear __Sir or Madam__,
I __wish__ to __complain__ about the coach trip __to__ __Hamburg__ on 3rd and 4th March. As a large __number__ of people had to __be__ __collected__ from different towns and __villages__ on the way, we were not able to take the 12 o'clock ferry as p__lanned__. As a r__esult__ of this there was no c__hance__ for me to go __sightseeing__ in Hamburg. In the hotel in Hamburg I was __not__ __given__ a single room, but had to __share__ a room with a man who was __unknown__ to me. As the coach was nowhere to __be found/seen__ outside the hotel, I was __forced__ to take the underground to the stadium, so I __arrived__ there half an hour after __the__ __match__ had __started__. In spite of having __booked__ and __paid__ for a seat on the grandstand[1], my seat was behind one of the goals, which __meant__ that I was not __able__ to see very well. At night it was nearly __impossible__ for me to sleep, as the hotel was located in a very __busy__ street. Finally, the breakfast in the morning was of __low__ q__uality__, too. In __view__ of all this, I __expect__ you to __refund__ part of the __sum__ I paid for the whole package and look __forward__ to __hearing__ from you very soon.
Yours __sincerely__, David Finch

[1] ['grændstæd] – Haupttribüne

## 4 Reading: American Idol

Complete the text – as shown in line 1 – with the words in the box.

| decide • young • laugh • people • in front of • audition • can't • popular • first • become • usually • call • best • their |

"American Idol" is a very __popular__ programme on American TV, and especially __young__ people love it. It is a talent contest[1] in which TV viewers can __call__ in and vote[2] for the performers to discover the singer with the most __best__ talent. In the __first__ round of the contest thousands of teenagers in cities all over the US. They have to sing a jury of three people who must __decide__ which of the hopeful young artists will make it to the second __in front of__ round. The jury members are quite strict[3], but sometimes they choose performers who __can't__ sing at all, __Usually__ because that makes it funnier for the __people__ who watch the show on TV! Some people have __become__ famous because __their__ performances were so bad that they made millions of TV viewers __laugh__ at them!

[1] ['kɒntest] – Wettbewerb • [2] [vəʊt] – (ab)stimmen, wählen • [3] [strɪkt] – streng

## 5 Mixed bag: The song contest[1]

Matt is talking to his friend about Marty McKenna, one of their classmates. Fill in the verbs in the correct tense – simple or progressive, active or passive. Sometimes you have to add *to* or a preposition, and there are negative forms, too.

Matt: Gary, __have__ you __read__ (read) the news about Marty in today's newspaper? He __'s going to sing__ (sing) in a song contest next month.
Gary: No, I __haven't had__ (have) a chance to read today's newspaper yet. But I __'ve been waiting for__ (wait) Marty since half past two. This morning he __said to__ (say) me that he __was going to meet__ (meet) his 'manager' Alex at two o'clock. After that, he __wanted to__ (want) come here, but so far he __hasn't arrived__ (arrive).
Matt: That's strange, because I __tried to call__ (try • call) him half an hour ago, but he __had already left__ (already • leave) his parents' house then. At least that's what I __was told__ (tell) by his mum. But Mrs McKenna __was__ (be) very busy. She __was making__ (make) dinner when I rang (ring).
Gary: Well, if Marty __isn't__ (be) here by six o'clock, I __'ll call__ (call) Alex, although I don't __like__ (like) him very much.

[1] ['kɒntest] – Wettbewerb

## 6 Mixed bag: British or American English?

Read the following extract from Linda's diary. She lives in a big city – but in which country? Underline the 27 words or phrases that tell you if she is British or American. Write down the "other" words, phrases or ways of spelling on the extra lines.

Dear diary,      Thursday, 12 Jan 2006

I've just come back from a great theatre and dance performance at school. It started at
__I just came__    __theater__    __in__
quarter past six and lasted until nine o'clock, but it was never boring. The dancers must have
__a quarter after six__
been practising for months, and our headteacher said that most of them had not even been on
__practicing__    __principal__
holiday since autumn. They were wearing special trousers with both legs a different colour.
__vacation__    __fall__    __pants__    __color__
That made a lot of the younger pupils laugh, but it is not the sort of humour I like. But the play
__students__    __kind__    __humor__
itself was great! My neighbour Sue was there, too. I'd gone by underground, but we took
__neighbor__    __subway__
a taxi home which Sue had called on her mobile. While we were waiting for it, we shared
__cab__    __cellphone__
a bag of chips. At the weekend, Sue's parents are going to London to watch a football match,
__fries__    __On__    __soccer__
so we can use their flat for a party! Sue said we could watch our favourite programmes on TV
__apartment__    __favorite programs__
and told me to bring some crisps. We haven't got any crisps at home, but I think
__chips__    __don't have__
sweets will be OK, too, and I've already taken some out of the cupboard in the kitchen.
__candy__    __I already took__
I'm really tired now, so I'll go to sleep.

# A song project

## 1 Speaking: Adverbs

Look at the following statements. Add one adverb of degree and one adverb of comment to each of them. Don't use any adverb more than once.

| utterly • of course • at all • apparently • completely • even • actually • really • absolutely • frankly • in fact • fortunately |

1. You're an ignorant person!
__Frankly__, you're a __really__ ignorant person!

2. You're bored by what I'm saying, aren't you?
__Apparently__ you're __completely__ bored by what I'm saying, aren't you?

3. I think you don't know the singer I'm talking about!
__Actually__ I think you don't __even__ know the singer I'm talking about.

4. You've no idea about music!
__In fact__ you've no idea about music __at all__!

5. I know you think I should change my style of music.
__Of course__ I know you think I should change my style of music __utterly__.

6. But I don't need your useless advice!
But __fortunately__ I don't need your __absolutely__ useless advice!

## 2 C-test: The talent show

Complete the missing words.

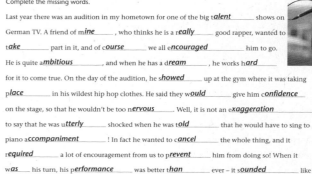

Last year there was an audition in my hometown for one of the big t__alent__ shows on German TV. A friend of m__ine__, who thinks he is a r__eally__ good rapper, wanted to t__ake__ part in it, and of c__ourse__ we all en__couraged__ him to go. He is quite am__bitious__, and when he has a d__ream__, he works h__ard__ for it to come true. On the day of the audition, he s__howed__ up at the gym where it was taking p__lace__ in his wildest hip hop clothes. He said they w__ould__ give him c__onfidence__ on the stage, so that he wouldn't be too n__ervous__. Well, it is not an ex__aggeration__ to say that he was u__tterly__ shocked when he was t__old__ that he would have to sing to piano ac__companiment__! In fact he wanted to c__ancel__ the whole thing, and it r__equired__ a lot of encouragement from us to p__revent__ him from doing so! When it w__as__ his turn, his p__erformance__ was better __than__ ever – it s__ounded__ like hip hop with a bit of Mozart! I'm c__onvinced__ that he will r__eceive__ a callback.

# Unit 5 text

## 3 Listening: Stage school audition

a) Before you listen to track 9, look at this information:

**Don't beat about the bush:** If somebody is taking too much time or too many words to say something.
**Get a move on:** Hurry up!

b) Now listen and tick (✔) the correct answer for each question. Be careful! The questions are not in the order you listened to them!

c) Listen again to check your answers.

1. Why doesn't Mike's dad go to school theatre performances?
   a) He doesn't like Shakespeare.
   b) He has to watch TV.
   ✔ c) He has no time.

2. What does Mike's mother think about Mike's plans?
   a) She's unhappy.
   b) She's scared.
   ✔ c) She's pleased.

3. At the audition Mike had to act some scenes. How many?
   ✔ a) Two.
   b) Three.
   c) Four.

4. What did Mike *not* have to do at the audition?
   a) He did not have to sing.
   ✔ b) He did not have to dance.
   c) He did not have to act.

5. Which college does Mike's dad want him to go to?
   a) The farming college.
   b) The business college.
   ✔ c) The teaching college.

6. Which museum did the boys go to?
   a) The British Museum.
   ✔ b) The Science Museum.
   c) The History Museum.

7. Where is Mike's stage school?
   a) It's in Birmingham.
   ✔ b) It's in London.
   c) It's in Liverpool.

8. What is Mike's dad's job?
   a) He's a teacher.
   ✔ b) He's a farmer.
   c) He's a vet.

## 4 Listening: A rock star

a) Listen carefully to track 10 and answer the following questions. b) Listen again to check your answers.

1. What is the name of Jazzie's rock band and who thought of it first?
*The band is called the "Thunderbirds" and (Jazzie's brother) Basher Jones thought of it.*

2. How many musicians are there in the band. What are their names?
*There are four musicians, (their names are) Basher, Shaker, Al, and Jazzie (who sings).*

3. What do most people think about rock stars?
*People think that rock stars can buy anything and do what they like.*

4. Why did Basher stop talking?
*He stopped talking because newspapers printed things (that) he hadn't said.*

5. What is one of the hardest things about being a rock star?
*One of the hardest things is that everyone is watching you all the time.*

6. What is bad about being on tour?
*It means that they spend six months on a tour bus and don't get enough sleep.*

7. What does the rock band do between tours?
*The rock band records new songs and appears on radio and TV.*

# Fame and fortune
## Unit 5 let's check

## 1 Grammar: Adverbs
Write the sentences again with the adverbs in the best positions.

1. Directors are not nice to teenage performers. (generally • really)
*(Generally) Directors are (generally) not really nice to teenage performers.*

2. So Tina was worried, although she had no reason to be. (absolutely • a bit)
*So Tina was a bit worried, although she had absolutely no reason to be.*

3. The singer who sang before her did not do well. (particularly • fortunately)
*Fortunately the singer who sang before her did not do particularly well.*

4. But Tina did not need any help, her performance was great! (simply • actually)
*But actually Tina did not need any help, her performance was simply great!*

## 2 Vocabulary: Word power   Complete the grid.

| Noun | Verb | Adjective | Adverb |
|---|---|---|---|
| appearance | to appear | apparent | apparently |
| completion | to complete | complete | completely |
| fortune | – | fortunate | fortunately |
| hope | to hope | hopeful | hopefully |
| luck | – | lucky | luckily |
| surprise | to surprise | a) *surprised* b) *surprising* | surprisingly |

## 3 Writing: Weekend activities   Put the words in the right order.

1. Marcus • sleeps • at the weekend • often • until 10 o'clock
*(At the weekend) Marcus often sleeps until 10 o'clock (at the weekend).*

2. Tina • goes • on Saturdays • usually • to the youth club
*(On Saturdays) Tina usually goes to the youth club (on Saturdays).*

3. Paul • visits • sometimes • on Sunday • his grandparents • in Leeds
*(Sometimes) (On Sundays) Paul (sometimes) visits his grandparents in Leeds (on Sundays).*

4. Clara • has • unfortunately • to work • once a month • at her aunt's hotel
*Unfortunately Clara has to work at her aunt's hotel once a month.*

# 3 focus
## Focus on international contacts

## 1 Mediation: Off to Australia on a Working Holiday Visa!

Lies die folgenden Informationen zu der Möglichkeit, Australien mit einem *Working Holiday Visa* zu erkunden. Schlage alle unbekannten Wörter nach, die du brauchst, um die wichtigen Details zu verstehen und beantworte dann die Fragen – auf Deutsch, aber mit Erklärungen!

**Working Holiday Makers**
The Working Holiday Program provides opportunities for people between 18 and 30 to holiday in Australia and to supplement their travel funds through incidental employment. Australia has reciprocal Working Holiday Maker arrangements in effect with the United Kingdom, Canada, the Netherlands, Japan, Republic of Ireland, Republic of Korea, Malta, Germany, Denmark, Sweden, Norway, the Hong Kong Special Administrative Region (HKSAR) of the People's Republic of China, Finland, the Republic of Cyprus, France, Italy, Belgium, Estonia and Taiwan. The visa allows a stay of up to 12 months from the date of first entry into Australia, regardless of whether or not you spend the whole time in Australia. You are allowed to do any kind of work of a temporary or casual nature, and you can work with each employer for up to three months. Working Holiday Makers who have worked as a seasonal worker in Regional Australia for a minimum of three months while on their first Working Holiday visa, will be eligible to apply for a second Working Holiday visa. Applicants need to demonstrate that they continue to meet the requirements for a Working Holiday visa. These include:
– being aged between 18 and 30
– having no dependents; and
– being a citizen of a country named in the Working Holiday Maker reciprocal arrangements. Seasonal work is defined as: picking fruit, nuts and other crops, […] and other work associated with packing or processing the harvest. Regional Australia includes anywhere in Australia except Sydney, Newcastle, Wollongong, the New South Wales Central Coast, Brisbane, the Gold Coast, Perth, Melbourne or the Australian Capital Territory. If you intend to apply for a second Working Holiday visa, you will need to provide evidence that you have worked for a minimum of three months as a seasonal worker in regional Australia while on your first Working Holiday visa. […] Acceptable evidence of seasonal work for Working Holiday Makers who undertook seasonal work in regional Australia may be original or certified copies of payslips … and other employer references. There are two ways to apply for the Working Holiday visa. They are:
– on the Internet
– by mail; you can download an application form from the official website of the Department of Immigration and Multicultural Affairs: www.immi.gov.au

1. Bekomme ich als Deutscher ein *Working Holiday Visa* (WHV)? *Ja, Abkommen mit der BRD.*

2. Wie kann ich ein *WHV* beantragen? *Im Internet oder per Post. Das Formular kann auf der angegebenen Website heruntergeladen werden.*

3. Wie lange ist ein *WHV* gültig? *12 Monate.*

4. Verlängert sich die Gültigkeitsdauer, wenn ich dazwischen drei Monate nach Neuseeland fliege?
*Nein, die Gültigkeit läuft durchgehend ab der ersten Einreise nach Australien.*

5. Mein Onkel ist 32 und möchte ein *WHV* beantragen. Geht das? *Nein, es können nur Personen zwischen 18 und 30 Jahren ein WHV beantragen.*

6. Kann ich ein halbes Jahr für einen Arbeitgeber arbeiten? *Nein, die Höchstdauer beträgt drei Monate bei einem Arbeitgeber.*

7. Wer kann nach Ablauf des ersten ein zweites *WHV* beantragen? *Alle Personen, die mit ihrem ersten WHV mindestens drei Monate als Erntehelfer gearbeitet haben.*

8. Kann man mit kleinen Kindern ein *WHV* beantragen? *Nein, Bewerber dürfen keine finanziell abhängigen Personen mitbringen.*

# 3 revision
## Up to Unit 5

## 1 Grammar: What if …?

Read the following sentences about animals in Australia. Rewrite them to say what would be / might be / would have been if things were / had been different.

1. Kangaroos have strong tails which help them to jump high in the air.
*If Kangaroos didn't have strong tails, they wouldn't be able to jump so high in the air.*

2. Koalas needn't drink water because they eat enough leaves.
*If Koalas didn't eat enough leaves, they would have to drink water.*

3. Wombats sleep during the day, so they are hardly ever spotted by tourists.
*If Wombats didn't sleep during the day, they would be spotted by tourists more often.*

4. Emus have always been hunted by the Aborigines because their meat tastes so good.
*If their meat didn't taste so good, Emus wouldn't always have been hunted by Aborigines.*

5. The Tasmanian tiger was hunted to extinction[1] because it ate the farmers' sheep.
*If the Tasmanian tiger hadn't eaten the farmers' sheep, it might not have been hunted to extinction.*

[1] [ɪkˈstɪŋkʃn] – Ausrottung

## 2 Grammar: Active or passive?

Fill in the verbs in the correct tense – active or passive, simple or progressive. Add *by* where necessary.

Last night Jack **was woken up by** (wake up) a loud noise in front of his bedroom window. When he **looked out** (look) out, he **saw** (see) that an accident **had happened** (happen). When he **opened** (open) the window, he **was asked by** (ask) a man if he had a telephone. Jack said, "Yes, of course", but a second later he **remembered** (remember) that he **had dropped** (drop) his phone on the floor the day before and it **hadn't been repaired** (not repair) yet. Suddenly the sound of an ambulance **could be heard** (could hear) – apparently it **had been called by** (call) the other driver. But in the end it **wasn't needed** (not need) because nobody **had been seriously injured** (injure • seriously) in the accident.

## 3 Grammar: Gerund or infinitive?

Complete the following story told by sixteen-year-old Carolyn, who moved from Melbourne to Cairns near the Great Barrier Reef after her mother had been offered a good job up there.
Fill in the gerund or the infinitive with *to*. Add prepositions where necessary.

After Mum and I had decided ___to leave___ (leave) Melbourne, we got really excited about ___going___ (go) up to Cairns ___to look___ (look) for a nice flat. Before we left, my mum told me ___not to forget___ (not forget) to say goodbye to my grandparents, and I suggested ___having___ (have) breakfast with them before we left. In fact, I was a little worried about ___leaving___ (leave) the two old people behind in Melbourne. But then the last words my grandma said to me before we left were, "And you know I don't want you ___to wear___ (wear) those mini-skirts," so that made things a little easier for me! How often she managed ___to drive___ (drive) me crazy with sentences like that! Our trip to Cairns was great, and it was hard ___to say___ (say) what was more fascinating: the ocean or the look on Mum's face. ___Being___ (be) together with her that day was great. She preferred ___driving___ (drive) all night ___to staying___ (stay) in a hotel, so we only stopped ___to get___ (get) gas and ___(to) take___ (take) pictures. After we had crossed the border into Queensland, she hardly stopped ___driving___ (drive) at all, and I didn't mind ___listening___ (listen) to all her stories. And suddenly I was not afraid of ___leaving___ (leave) my friends in Melbourne any more, but was already looking forward to ___making___ (make) new ones in Cairns.

# Perfektes Sprachtraining, gute Noten, super Preis:
## die Schülersoftware zu Green Line NEW Bayern

**39,95 €**

**Sprachtrainer Englisch Band 4**
Die Vollversion der Schülersoftware passend zu Green Line NEW Bayern ist deine multimediale Workstation für zu Hause mit Grammatiktrainer, Vokabeltrainer und Kommunikationstrainer.
Einzelversion   978-3-12-990524-1   € 39,95
Preise freibleibend Stand Juli 2006

**Erhältlich im Buchhandel oder unter www.klett.de**
Ernst Klett Verlag, Postfach 10 26 45, 70022 Stuttgart
Telefon 07 11 · 66 72-13 33, Telefax 07 11 · 66 72-20 80

# GREEN LINE NEW
## Bayern 4

Trainingsbuch Schulaufgaben

LEARNING ENGLISH GREEN LINE NEW

BAYERN

Das Lösungsheft ist ein Bestandteil von
ISBN-10: 3-12-**547273**-3
ISBN-13: 978-3-12-**547273**-0

# Inhaltsverzeichnis für den Übungsteil

Vorwort für Schülerinnen, Schüler und Eltern .................... 2

Unit 1 .................... 4

Focus 1 .................... 15

Unit 2 .................... 17

Revision 1 .................... 27

Unit 3 .................... 28

Focus 2 .................... 39

Unit 4 .................... 40

Revision 2 .................... 51

Unit 5 .................... 52

Focus 3 .................... 62

Revision 3 .................... 63

# Inhaltsverzeichnis für die Hör-CD (hinten im Trainingsbuch eingeklebt)

| Track | Unit | Typ | Titel | Sprechzeit |
|---|---|---|---|---|
| 1 | 1 | Listening | The weather forecast | 3' 11" |
| 2 | 1 | Listening | Gold-mining in Western Australia | 3' 15" |
| 3 | 2 | Listening | Booking a ghost tour in London | 4' 46" |
| 4 | 2 | Listening | Cornish ghosts | 3' 21" |
| 5 | 3 | Listening | A short history of Scottish tartan | 2' 47" |
| 6 | 3 | Listening | Museums in Edinburgh | 4' 04" |
| 7 | 4 | Listening | An interesting job | 4' 16" |
| 8 | 4 | Listening | A short history of the Mayflower | 3' 52" |
| 9 | 5 | Listening | Stage school audition | 3' 58" |
| 10 | 5 | Listening | A rock star | 3' 53" |

Gesamtdauer: 37' 58"

# Vorwort

Liebe Schülerinnen und Schüler,

das **Trainingsbuch Schulaufgaben** besteht aus drei Teilen:

> 1. dem **Übungsteil**,
> 2. dem **Lösungsheft** mit allen Lösungen,
> 3. der **Hör-CD** mit den Hörverstehenstexten.

Der **Übungsteil** enthält Übungen zu den folgenden Lernbereichen:

▶ **Vocabulary**
mit Übungen zum Wortschatz

▶ **Grammar**
mit Übungen zur Grammatik

▶ **Speaking**
mit Übungen zum Training der Sprechfertigkeit

▶ **Writing**
mit Übungen zur Schulung des Schreibens

▶ **Mediation**
mit Übungen zur Übertragung ins Englische

▶ **Reading**
mit Übungen zum Textverstehen

▶ **Cloze test / C-test**
Texte mit Wortschatzlücken bzw. mit Wortanfängen in regelmäßigen Abständen

▶ **Mixed bag / Error-spotting**
Übungen zu Wortschatz und Grammatik mit Fehlerkorrektur

▶ **Listening**
mit Übungen zum Hörverstehen

Vor jeder Übung steht, was besonders geübt wird, z. B. **1 Vocabulary: Odd word out**. Möchtet ihr die Grammatik oder das Übertragen ins Englische üben, findet ihr geeignete Übungen unter **Grammar** und **Mediation**. Möchtet ihr noch einen Lückentext üben oder ausprobieren, ob ihr die Vokabeln gut könnt, wählt ihr **Mixed bag, Cloze test** und die Übungen zu **Vocabulary**.

Das **Lösungsheft** enthält alle Seiten des Übungsteils in verkleinerter Form und mit den eingetragenen Lösungen. Hier könnt ihr alle Lösungen schnell und übersichtlich nachschauen. Wenn mehrere Lösungen richtig sind, sind diese auch eingetragen. Bei freien Übungen sind die Lösungen natürlich nur Vorschläge.

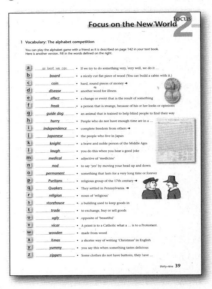

Beispielseite aus dem Lösungsheft mit eingetragenen Lösungen

Die **Hör-CD** enthält die Hörverstehenstexte. Die Tracknummer ist bei den jeweiligen Übungen im Übungsteil angegeben. Ihr müsst nur darauf achten, dass ihr die richtige Tracknummer ansteuert. Die Hörverstehenstexte gibt es nur auf der CD, denn sie sind ausschließlich zum Hören gedacht.

Das **Trainingsbuch Schulaufgaben** ist genauso aufgebaut wie das Schülerbuch und das **Workbook**. Auf jeder Seite oben ist ein Hinweis, auf welchen Teil des Schülerbuchs sich die Übungen beziehen, z. B. **Unit 2 Language A.**

Diese Gliederung kennt ihr bereits aus dem Schülerbuch und auch aus dem **Workbook**, also nichts Neues für euch. Natürlich kann man nie ganz genau wissen, was in einer Schulaufgabe wirklich drankommt und jede Lehrerin / jeder Lehrer stellt die Schulaufgaben ein klein wenig anders. Aber für euch ist es wichtig zu wissen, dass die Lernbereiche, die in den Schulaufgaben vorkommen können, hier im **Trainingsbuch** auch geübt werden. Die einzige Ausnahme ist die freie Textproduktion (*creative writing*), weil ihr dazu eine Rückmeldung von eurer Lehrerin / eurem Lehrer braucht.

# Vorwort

Das **Trainingsbuch Schulaufgaben** könnt ihr folgendermaßen benutzen:

**1.** Zur Vorbereitung auf eine Schulaufgabe: Wenn eure Lehrerin/euer Lehrer z.B. sagt: Die nächste Schulaufgabe geht von Unit 2 bis Unit 3 einschließlich, dann solltet ihr euch im **Trainingsbuch** die Übungen zu Unit 2 und Unit 3 vornehmen und sie möglichst **alle** durcharbeiten. Durch die Anordnung der Übungen könnt ihr sicher sein, dass ihr alle wichtigen Übungsformen mindestens einmal geübt habt. Dann kann eigentlich nichts mehr schief gehen!

**2.** Zum zusätzlichen Üben zwischen den Schulaufgaben: In diesem Fall könnt ihr nach der Durchnahme eines Abschnitts im Schülerbuch überprüfen, ob ihr den Stoff wirklich beherrscht. Wichtig ist dabei: Das **Trainingsbuch** bitte erst benutzen, **nachdem** ihr den entsprechenden Teil im Schülerbuch durchgenommen habt!

**Wie übt ihr am besten?**

Am besten übt ihr natürlich regelmäßig und nicht erst kurz vor einer Schulaufgabe. Denn nur so habt ihr Zeit, einen Abschnitt oder einen Lernbereich noch einmal gründlich zu wiederholen, wenn er noch nicht sitzt. Nehmt euch regelmäßig eine oder zwei Übungen vor, sobald ihr ein Kapitel im Schülerbuch abgeschlossen habt. Überprüft mit Hilfe des **Lösungshefts**, ob eure Antworten richtig sind. Es hat aber keinen Zweck, die Lösungen aus dem Lösungsheft abzuschreiben. Ihr könnt mit euren Eltern z.B. vereinbaren, dass ihr das Lösungsheft abgebt und erst hineinschaut, wenn ihr die Übungen durchgeführt habt. Vergleicht dann eure Lösungen mit dem Lösungsheft und verbessert eure Fehler.

Bei allen Übungen, die im Übungsteil ein CD-Symbol am Rand haben, braucht ihr die **Hör-CD**, die hinten im **Trainingsbuch** eingeklebt ist. Hört euch die Hörtexte zunächst immer einmal vollständig an. Lest danach die Aufgabe im Übungsteil durch und hört die Aufnahme ein zweites (und drittes) Mal. Bearbeitet jetzt die Übung und überprüft eure Ergebnisse entweder mit dem Text im Lösungsteil oder hört zur Kontrolle noch einmal die CD.

Wenn einmal ein oder zwei Fehler vorkommen, dann ist das nicht so schlimm. Wenn sich aber die Fehler häufen, dann müsst ihr etwas tun, z.B. noch einmal die Vokabeln lernen oder in der Grammatik im Schülerbuch nachschauen oder die eine oder andere Übung im **Schülerbuch**, **Workbook** oder in der Software **Sprachtrainer Englisch** wiederholen.

Wir wünschen euch viel Erfolg mit dem **Trainingsbuch Schulaufgaben**.

# Down under

## 1 Vocabulary: Australian wildlife

**Across →**
1. Animals with eight legs.
2. It is not really a bear.
3. A really cute animal.
4. Many Australian snakes are very …
5. These birds can't fly.
6. This animal can jump.
7. In some parts of Australia, you should not go swimming in rivers, as they are full of …
8. Bites from some of the (see 1.) that live in Australia can be …
9. … are fish with very sharp teeth.

**Down ↓**
10. Nickname[1] for Australia.

[1]['nɪkneɪm] – Spitzname

## 2 Mixed bag: Error-spotting

There are two mistakes in each line of the following text. Underline them and write down the correct words on the right.

Australia is the dryest continent. In most part's of the outback, _____

their is very little rain. This is one reason because most people _____

living on or near the coast. There are huge cow stations in _____

the outback, and Australia has more sheeps then people, too. _____

Sydney is the bigest city in the country with about four millions _____

inhabitents. It's most famous landmarks are the Opera House _____

and the Harbour bridge, and Bondi Beach is Sydney's popularest _____

beach. Sydneysiders[1] are realy keen of swimming and other _____

water sports, so in Summer there are always a lots of people on _____

the city's many wonderfull beachs. _____

[1]['sɪdneɪˌsaɪdəz] – people who live in Sydney

4 four

# New neighbours

**language A** — unit 1

## 1 Writing: What did Matt say?

**a)** Matt told and asked Lin a lot of things.

1. "Where did you live before you moved to Sydney?"
2. "My parents bought our house when I was a baby."
3. "You should come over to our place tomorrow."
4. "How long has your family been living in Australia?"
5. "In summer we often have barbecues in our garden."
6. "I hope you'll go to my school."
7. "There are a lot of nice people in my class."
8. "Have you met my parents?"

**b)** The next day Lin told her family what Matt had said or asked. Use the following verbs:

want to know (2x)    ask    mention    tell    point out    say (2x)

1. Lin: Matt _____
2. He _____
3. _____
4. _____
5. _____
6. _____
7. _____
8. _____

## 2 C-test: Asians in Australia      Complete the missing words.

The Wangs are new in Rockdale, a s_____ of Sydney. Like the Wangs, a lot of Sydney's four million i_____ were born in Asia. They came to Australia as i_____ from China, Malaysia, Thailand, Indonesia and other P_____ Rim countries. Most of these people didn't _____ time after they had a_____ in Australia, but started to _____ hard immediately. They didn't d_____ that they could 'make it' there, they b_____ in their own success. Of course, Australia is a very important t_____ partner for most Asian countries, so many Asians who come to Australia work for c_____ from their home countries.

five 5

# unit 1 language A

## 3 Grammar: What Lin would like Matt to do

When the Wangs were saying goodbye to the Donovans, Lin said many things to Matt. Use indirect commands and the following verbs to report what she said.

tell   advise   want   invite   ask   warn

1. "You can come and visit me any time."

_____

2. "It's best to knock at our door, as the door bell doesn't work."

_____

3. "But stay away from Lizzy, our cat."

_____

4. "It would be great if you brought some of your favourite CDs."

_____

5. "Could you let me have a look at the books you use at school?"

_____

6. "Please don't come over before 10 o'clock on Sundays."

_____

## 4 Speaking: Ms Beumer

After school Lin reported a conversation with her teacher to her mother.

> Today I was asked by my Maths teacher, Ms Beumer if I had learned to speak English in China. So I told her I hadn't, as I'd never been to China! She said she was sorry, and explained to me that she had an Asian student in another class who'd only been living in Australia for a year, but already spoke perfect English. I told her that we'd only just moved to Sydney, so that's why I was new there. Then she told me not to worry, as that was a good school, and asked me if there was anything she could do for me. But I said I was fine and added that I'd come back to her when I needed help.

Now write down Lin's conversation with her teacher. Add words to make it sound better where necessary.

Ms Beumer: _____

Lin: _____

Ms Beumer: _____

_____

_____

Lin: _____

Ms Beumer: _____

_____

Lin: _____

**6**  six

## 5 Mediation: Can you tell me the way to …, please?

One day Matt's classmate Rob met a German tourist in downtown Sydney. As Rob's parents are from Nuremberg[1], Rob speaks German.

*Tourist:* Entschuldigung, sprichst du Deutsch?
*Rob:* Ja, das tue ich, Sie haben Glück.
*Tourist:* Wohnst du hier?
*Rob:* Naja, ich wohne nicht im Stadtzentrum, sondern in einem Vorort.
*Tourist:* Aber du weißt, wie man zum Opernhaus kommt, oder?
*Rob:* Na klar, weiß ich das.
*Tourist:* Bitte sag es mir!
*Rob:* Gehen Sie diese Straße entlang, bis Sie zu einem Souvenirgeschäft kommen. Biegen Sie dort nach rechts ab und wenden Sie sich an der nächsten Straße nach links. Nach etwa 100 Metern sehen Sie das Opernhaus.
*Tourist:* Vielen Dank. Warum sprichst du so gut Deutsch?
*Rob:* Meine Eltern kamen vor 20 Jahren als Einwanderer aus Deutschland hierher.
*Tourist:* Sag Ihnen, dass du einen Rainer aus Schweinfurt getroffen hast.
*Rob:* Das mache ich. Wiedersehen.

[1] ['njʊərəmbɜːg] – Nürnberg

Later Rob reported this conversation to Matt. Use the following verbs:

`explain`   `say`   `ask`   `want to know`   `tell`   `answer`   `advise`

*Rob:* Today I met a tourist in George Street. I don't know why, but he asked me if I spoke German. Do I look German? Well, I said _____ and _____ him he _____. So he _____ I _____ _____ He asked me _____ _____ House. I _____ asked me to tell him.

I _____ souvenir shop. I _____ _____ I _____ _____ metres.

He said thanks and _____

I _____ _____

So he _____

I _____ before I said goodbye to him.

# Unit 1 language B

# An experience in the outback

## 1 Grammar: If things had been different …

Which words on the right go well with the if-clauses on the left? Finish the sentences as in the example.

1. If Matt had grown up in the outback,

   he would have learned to throw a boomerang.

   | not take back | Matt | house |

2. If Jack hadn't grown up in the outback,

   _____

   | learn | throw | boomerang |

3. If the snake hadn't been poisonous,

   _____

   | Matt | transport | hospital |

4. If Jack's dad hadn't had a 4WD[1],

   _____

   | Jack | laugh at | cousin |

5. If the Flying Doctors hadn't got Jack's call,

   _____

   | not recognize | snake | Matt |

[1]4WD = short for Four-Wheel-Drive – Geländewagen

## 2 Grammar: Which type of conditional?

Choose the right form to make conditional sentences.

1. **If the weather is good tomorrow, …**
   a) I will go to the beach.
   b) I would go to the beach.
   c) I would have gone to the beach.

2. **I would have gone swimming every day …**
   a) if I am not ill last week.
   b) if I wasn't ill last week.
   c) if I hadn't been ill last week.

3. **If we lived in the north of Australia, …**
   a) we can go surfing every day.
   b) we could go surfing every day.
   c) we could have gone surfing every day.

4. **I would go surfing more often …**
   a) if I don't have so much homework to do.
   b) if I didn't have so much homework to do.
   c) if I hadn't had so much homework to do.

5. **If Sydney didn't have so many immigrants, …**
   a) it will be a lot less interesting.
   b) it would be a lot less interesting.
   c) it would have been a lot less interesting.

6. **I wouldn't be so nervous now …**
   a) if I don't meet Lin yesterday.
   b) if I didn't meet Lin yesterday.
   c) if I hadn't met Lin yesterday.

## 3 Grammar: What if ...?

Read the following text and make sentences to say what would/might/could happen or have happened if things were/had been different.

Be careful – some sentences are different from the basic types of conditionals.

Robert from Germany went on a working holiday to Australia for half a year in 2006.

1. Robert's English was good, so he wasn't worried.

2. He didn't have to take the bus from Sydney Airport because he had met a nice boy on the plane.

3. The boy's parents live in central Sydney, so they gave him a lift.

4. When Robert told them the name of his hotel, they invited him to their house (it's a bad hotel).

5. Robert left after two weeks, because his new friend, Alex, had to go back to school.

6. Alex's father, Mr Linsley, is a tourist guide, so he travels a lot.

7. Mr Linsley knows a lot of important people, so he was able to help Robert find a job.

8. Alex has the same hobbies as Robert so they still send each other e-mails.

# unit 1 language B

## 4 Reading: How to 'make' water in the desert

**a)** Perhaps you know that koalas needn't drink water because they eat enough leaves from trees. Of course we humans do need water, but this doesn't mean we're lost if we forget to take enough of it on a trip in the Australian outback. Read the following instructions from an Australian survival handbook. Even though you probably do not know every single word, you should be able to understand the method that is described.

**b)** Nun fertige eine einfache Profilskizze an, die dir hilft, einem Freund oder einer Freundin das, was du soeben gelesen hast, zu erklären. Beschrifte sie auf Deutsch!

**How to to get water with the help of plastic sheeting[1]**

One of the ways of getting water in the bush is by using plastic sheeting. If you always carry a few pieces of heavy plastic, each about 1 m² in size, you will be able to collect about half a litre of water a day per sheet. In an emergency, any type of plastic – a raincoat or a bag – can be used.

**This is how to do it:** For each sheet, dig a hole in the ground, about 60 x 60 cm square and about 45 cm deep. Fill the bottom 10 cm of the hole with green leaves and branches from the trees around the place where you have set up camp; put a container of some sort in the middle – a cup is a bit too small!

Cover the hole with a plastic sheet and seal the edges with dirt to make it as airtight as possible.

In the middle of the sheet, place a stone heavy enough to make the plastic bulge towards the container.

With the heat of the sun, moisture[2] will slowly be drawn from the leaves and the ground, and will condense on the underside of the plastic. The water will then run down the slope made by the stone and drip into the container.

**Note:** The next day you must make the hole 3–4 cm deeper and put new leaves inside.

[1]['plæstɪk 'ʃiːtɪŋ] – Plastikfolie • [2]['mɔɪstʃə] – Feuchtigkeit

## 5 Listening: Weather forecasting

**a)** Listen to track 1 and choose the correct answer to the questions. **b)** Listen again and check your answers.

1. Barny works at a weather station in
   a) Austria.   b) Australia.

2. What's the weather like in Manchester?
   a) It's raining.   b) It isn't raining.

3. The sunniest capital in Australia is
   a) Sydney   b) Melbourne
   c) Darwin

4. How many hours of sunshine does Melbourne get?
   a) 5.5 hours   b) 6.7 hours
   c) 7.5 hours   d) 5.7 hours

5. On how many days of the year does it rain in Waratah?
   a) 214   b) 340
   c) 314

6. Snow falls in Australia above
   a) 1500 metres   b) 1300 metres
   c) 1600 metres

7. People visit the Australian Alps because the area is
   a) a natural park   b) a national park
   c) an international park

8. What's surprising? Canberra is
   a) the wettest city.   b) the cleanest city.
   c) the foggiest city.

## 6 Mediation: The outback

Lisa (15) ist mit ihren Eltern und ihrer 10-jährigen Schwester Clara zu Besuch auf einer Schaffarm im australischen Outback. Die beiden Mädchen sind auf einem Rundgang mit dem Sohn des Farmers und dessen Hund. Da Jeff (16) kein Deutsch und Clara kaum Englisch spricht, muss Lisa für die beiden dolmetschen. Benutze *if*-Sätze in Lisas Übertragungen.

*Clara:* Wir müssen jetzt wieder zurück, sonst fahren Mama und Papa ohne uns ab.

*Lisa:* She says if we don't go back now, Mum and Dad will leave without us.

*Jeff:* Well, if you hadn't wanted to go so far out, we wouldn't have to hurry now.

*Lisa:* Er sagt, wenn _____

_____

*Clara:* Gut, dass wir den Hund dabei haben, sonst würden wir nie zum Haus zurückfinden.

*Lisa:* She says if _____

_____

*Jeff:* Rubbish! I wouldn't have taken you girls out here if our lives had depended on my old dog.

*Lisa:* Er sagt, _____

_____

*Clara:* Wenn ich euch sagen müsste, wo das Haus ist, hätte ich keine Chance.

*Lisa:* She says _____

_____

*Jeff:* Well, if you'd lived here for more than ten years, you would know where to go, too.

*Lisa:* Er sagt, wenn _____

_____

*Clara:* Unmöglich! Und außerdem – wenn er mir vorher gesagt hätte, dass hier alles gleich aussieht, wäre ich gar nicht mitgekommen.

*Lisa:* She says that's _____ ! And if _____

_____

*Jeff:* Well, if she had asked me, I would have told her. Tell her to watch out for snakes and crocodiles on the way back.

*Lisa:* Er sagt, _____

_____

*Clara:* Aaaaaah!

# Rabbit-proof fence

## 1 Cloze test: How the kangaroo got its tail (based on an Australian Aboriginal legend)

Complete the text with suitable words.

A long _____ ago, Kareela the Kangaroo and Wambiri the Wombat lived _____ in a hut. They liked being with _____ other, but Kareela liked _____ sleep outside at night and he _____ fun of Wambiri, who always _____ to sleep inside. "Come on, Wambiri, _____ outside with me," said Kareela. "It's much nicer to _____ up at the stars at night and listen to the fresh wind in the trees." "It's too _____ outside," said Wambiri, "and sometimes it _____. I might _____ wet! I like sleeping in my hut with a nice fire to keep me warm." When winter came, the wind _____ colder at night. At first Kareela didn't _____. He _____ himself that the wind couldn't _____ him – he wasn't afraid. When it _____ to rain, he said "a little wind and rain _____ hurt me. I'm not afraid." But one night, Kareela was so _____ and cold, he _____ take it any longer. He got up and _____ on Wambiri's door. "It's me!" screamed Kareela. "Now, _____ me in!" "No!" shouted Wambiri. "There isn't _____ room." Kareela became very _____ and pushed hard at the _____ until it opened. "I'm _____ now – and you aren't big enough to _____ me out!" – "Well, sleep _____ there – in the corner," said Wambiri and _____ back to sleep near the fire. Kareela _____ down in the corner, but _____ was a hole in the wall of the _____ and the wind and rain came in. He couldn't dry _____ or get warm. In the _____ he felt terrible. He went outside and _____ up a large rock. Wambiri was just _____ up when Kareela dropped the _____ on his head. "That's for _____ helping me get warm and dry," said Kareela. "And _____ now on, you'll always _____ in a cold, dark hole." After that, Wambiri and Kareela didn't _____ to each other or play together, and Wambiri planned his _____. He made a big spear and _____ until Kareela was washing _____. Then he _____ the spear, and it _____ the kangaroo at the base of his spine[1]. Kareela screamed in pain and tried to _____ the spear out, but he couldn't. "From now on, that _____ be your long tail," shouted Wambiri, "and you'll _____ have a home to live in!" That is _____ wombats now have flat foreheads[2] and live in dark, damp burrows[3] and why kangaroos have long _____ and always sleep outside, under the stars.

[1] [spaɪn] – Steißbein • [2] ['fɒrɪd] – Stirn • [3] [ˌdʌmp 'bʌrəʊ] – feuchter Bau

## 2 Listening: Gold-mining in Western Australia

**a)** Before listening to track 2 look at these words and their definitions.

**Gold-mining** is going underground to find gold.
**Gold fields** are places where you can find gold in the ground.
**Grasslands** are places to keep cattle.
**The Gold Rush** was when a lot of people from Australia and other parts of the world went to look for gold.
An **ounce** of gold is about 31 grams.
A **claim** is registered by someone who finds gold and says that they want to look for more at one certain place
A **pipeline** is a long pipe to transport water or oil a long way.
A **mile** is 1.6 kilometres.

**b)** Now complete the puzzle with the words above. There are no spaces between the words.

1. Where farmers keep their cattle in Australia.
2. This is made by someone who finds gold somewhere and wants people to know he was there first.
3. This was what happened when a lot of people went to find gold.
4. A way of measuring how far away a place is.
5. This carries water from a reservoir to a town or city.
6. This is where people found gold.
7. 31 grams of gold are about an … of gold.
8. The name of the metal in the puzzle.

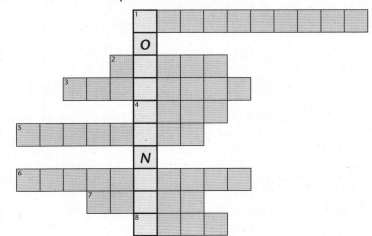

**c)** Listen to track 2 twice. Here are some of the numbers the text talks about. Decide if the definition of each number is true or false.

| | | true | false |
|---|---|---|---|
| 1. **1863** | The first man rode over the gold fields in Western Australia. | ☐ | ☐ |
| 2. **1864–68** | A man named C.C. Hunt crossed the gold fields. | ☐ | ☐ |
| 3. **500–1000** | This much money in pounds was given to the last person to find gold. | ☐ | ☐ |
| 4. **554** | This is the amount of gold in ounces found in a town called Coolgardie. | ☐ | ☐ |
| 5. **1893** | Three Irishmen started looking for gold in Western Australia. | ☐ | ☐ |
| 6. **1903** | A pipeline brought oil to the gold-miners. | ☐ | ☐ |
| 7. **557** | The length of the pipeline in miles. | ☐ | ☐ |
| 8. **35,000,000** | The weight of gold in ounces found in Kalgoorlie gold mines since 1893. | ☐ | ☐ |

**d)** Listen again and check your answers. If you got them all right first time, that's very good!

# unit 1
### let's check

## 1 Reading: Christmas down under

Complete the text – as shown in line 1 – with the words below.

wear — to — kids — if — called — what — cards — it — until
but — pieces — visit — barbecue — from — popular — so — never — box

Australians celebrate Christmas, too, but is very different Christmas in Europe or North America. Of
                                            it

course Christmas down under is white, especially as it is in summer. Temperatures are about 25 to
38 degrees Celcius, most Australians have their parties outdoors, for example with a real Australian !
Picnics on the beach are very _____, too, and it is great to see Aussies take _____ down to the beach on Christmas
Day: whole turkeys, huge _____ of ham, large bowls of salad, cakes, puddings and at least one esky, a large
plastic _____ to keep drinks cool, per person. Santa Claus doesn't _____ Australia on a sleigh that is pulled by
reindeer, he comes on a surfboard that is pulled by six white kangaroos which are _____ 'boomers'! And of
course it is much too hot to _____ a coat, so Santa has a red T-shirt and shorts on! For Australian _____ Christmas is
the best time of the year not only because they get presents, _____ also because it's the time of their longest
holidays, which last six weeks _____ the end of January. But there are things which are very similar to
Christmas in Europe or North America. Children write _____ or letters to Santa Claus with the things they
would like to have. Many people go _____ church on Christmas Eve. People put up Christmas decorations,
and many families have a 'Christmas tree' – even _____ it's only a branch from a gumtree[1]!

[1] ['gʌmtri:] – Eukalyptusbaum

## 2 C-test: Rabbit-proof fence    Complete the missing words.

First the sound of the plane r_____ Daisy of the Flying Doctors, who came to her village
three or four t_____ a year. But when she saw that it was c_____ above them, she knew
it meant d_____ , because the people in it were probably l_____ down to find three
little r_____ girls. Planes were much worse than all the s_____ parties with dogs and
horses. They had to follow their f_____ , which had been washed away by the rain. But from
the _____ they were easy to see, because in the d_____ there were large areas without any
t_____ and it was impossible to find s_____ . But this time they _____ lucky –
there were some big trees straight _____ of them, so they ran, climbed up and h_____ under
the branches. After some minutes, the plane _____ up, and the girls walked on in s_____ .

# Focus on the Golden Age

## 1 Reading: The Spanish Armada

It was a hot evening in July, 1588. All was quiet in Plymouth harbour where the English ships <u>lay</u> at <u>anchor</u>. Everybody, however, knew it was the <u>calm</u> before the storm because the Great Armada was waiting to attack England. On that evening Sir Francis Drake and a few other officers had gone to play bowls when the news was brought that the Spanish ships had been <u>spotted</u> in the English Channel.

Drake had a plan in mind, but he wanted to finish the game he was playing before he put his plan into action. He let the 130 huge Spanish ships with 30,000 men on board sail up the Channel before attacking them from the <u>rear</u>. Then the British ships, only half the size of the Spanish ones, <u>fired</u> their guns and turned away quickly before the enemy could return the fire.

Eventually the Spanish <u>cast</u> anchor just off Calais, a place they thought to be safe. But Drake knew how to force them out to sea again: The British filled their ships with <u>pitch</u>, set fire to them and let them <u>drift</u> towards the Spanish, who cut their ropes and sailed off in great chaos. A <u>fierce</u> storm drove them north to Scotland and Ireland where most of the ships were lost in heavy seas. Only fifty-four of them returned to Spain.

a) Use your dictionary to find the correct meaning of the underlined words.

| Word in the text | Dictionary | German |
|---|---|---|
| lay | vi: to lie — lay — lain | liegen — lag — gelegen |
| anchor | | |
| calm | | |
| spotted | | |
| rear | | |
| fired | | |
| cast | | |
| pitch | | |
| drift | | |
| fierce | | |

b) Find synonyms for these words in the text.

eventually –

cast –

off –

c) Find opposites from the text.

tiny –

front –

gentle –

# focus 1

## 2 Vocabulary: Guess who I am

All these people lived between 1400 and 1600. They give you a clue so that you can guess who they are.

1. I think people should live according to the moral values of the Bible.
2. I'm from Devon and I sailed around the world in my ship "The Golden Hinde".
3. I'm German and I invented the printing press.
4. Once I was Queen, but I was executed when my husband wanted to take a new wife.
5. I never married because I wanted to serve my country as Queen.
6. I'm good at writing drama and poems. I hope my Queen likes it.
7. I'm an Italian lady in a famous picture.
8. I think there is too much ceremony in the Catholic church, we should have some changes.
9. I painted the famous picture of the Italian lady.
10. I wanted to find a new route to India, but actually landed at the other side of the world.
11. I'm the king who married six times to have a son, but in the end my daughter became Queen.

## 3 Vocabulary: Word families

a) Make adjectives from these nouns.

| gold | |
| wealth | |
| value | |
| poison | |
| crowd | |
| danger | |
| death | |

b) Make nouns from these verbs.

| to settle | |
| to speak | |
| to influence | |
| to sail | |
| to colonize | |
| to print | |
| to explore | |

# On the southwestern coast

intro

## 1 Vocabulary: Crossword puzzle

**Down** ↓
1. A Devon town with a famous cathedral.
2. A small bay.
3. A place where ghosts are believed to be is …
5. A town near Land's End.
7. A person who visits interesting places.
8. Here you find a museum of smuggling.
9. Something you can find on the "Jurassic Coast".
12. A drink produced in Devon.

**Across** →
4. The port Sir Francis Drake sailed from against the Armada.
6. King Arthur's legendary birthplace.
10. The Gulf Stream makes the … in Cornwall mild.
11. Wild ponies live here.
13. The south coast of Cornwall is called the "English …".

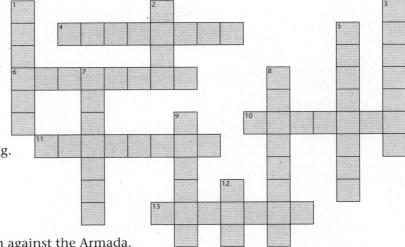

## Paradise on earth

language A

### 1 Grammar: On Saturday at 11 o'clock in Torquay

Write what is happening in the pictures. Use passive forms in the present progressive.

1. Fruit and vegetables _____are being sold_____ (sell) at the market.

2. Boats _____ (push) into the sea.

3. Sails _____ (put up) by two young men.

4. Restaurant tables _____ (set) for lunch.

5. Mrs Pierce _____ (ask) the way by a tourist.

An hour later: Write passive sentences in the present perfect.

1. Most of the fruit _____has been sold_____ .

2. The boats _____ into the water. They are out at sea now.

3. The sails _____ and the two men have sailed away.

4. The tables _____ and the first guests have arrived.

5. The tourist's questions _____ and Mrs Pierce has gone home.

seventeen **17**

## 2 Speaking: Visiting the Eden Project

Tobias and Edith, two German pupils who are doing a two-week language course at a language school near Exeter are visiting the Eden Project. They are asking a guide about the project. Write the guide's answers in the correct tense. Use passive forms.

1. Is it true that people call the Eden project a world wonder?

   Yes, it _____ **(sometimes • refer to)** as the eighth wonder of the world.

2. Where did the money for the project come from?

   Well, most of the project _____ **(pay for)** with lottery money, but part of it _____ **(earn)** from visitors like you.

3. I've heard that they made a James Bond movie here in Eden.

   That's true. "The other day" with Pierce Brosnan _____ **(film)** here.

4. Where did you get the plants from?

   Actually, most of the plants _____ **(grow)** from seeds and not _____ **(take)** from the wild.

5. What exactly does the Eden Project want the visitors to learn?

   Well, the visitors _____ **(teach)** here about the natural world. They _____ **(show)** how natural resources _____ **(have to • save)** so that they _____ **(can • use)** in the future.

6. Could you tell us how you use the rain water that falls on the roof?

   Of course it is _____ **(use)** to water the plants, and the mist _____ **(create)** with it. But also the toilets _____ **(flush)** with it.

7. We've seen so many buses outside. What do you do when there are too many visitors?

   That's really a problem. Once or twice our gates _____ **(close)** so that visitors had to wait to _____ **(let in)**.

## 3 Vocabulary: Working with the dictionary

Take your dictionary and find out how the words on the right can be used.

contain   display   refer to   environment
label   remove   Mediterranean   humid
damage   resources   rare   seed

1. Four words can be nouns and verbs: <u>display,</u> _____

2. Two words are only adjectives: _____

3. Which words are only nouns? _____

4. Which words are only verbs? _____

5. Which word can be an adjective and a noun? _____

## 4 Grammar: After the storm

Mr Burton was away in London when the storm hit his little village at the seaside.
Use the past progressive form of the passive to describe what was being done, when he got home.

1. An old man _____ was being carried _____ (carry) into an ambulance.

2. A little boy _____ (examine) by a doctor, while his brother, who was still missing, _____ (look for) by some village people.

3. Some chairs _____ (take back) to the café.

4. A big tree _____ (remove) from the street.

5. A damaged car _____ (tow) to the garage to be repaired.

6. Photos _____ (take) by a photographer and his neighbour _____ (interview) by a journalist.

# Two men in a boat

## 1 Grammar: At the tourist office

Susan works at the tourist office in Penzance. People come to her with their questions and problems.
Change their statements by using the personal passive.

| Somebody told me that there is a bus to Land's End. Can you tell me where it leaves from? | _____ that there is a bus to Land's End. Can you tell me where it leaves from? |

| Nobody told us that there is a rock concert near our hotel on Saturday. Do you think we can move to another hotel? | _____ that there is a rock concert near our hotel on Saturday. Do you think we can move to another hotel? |

| Someone asked me if I want to go to the rock concert with him. Do you know where I can buy a ticket? | _____ if I want to go to the rock concert. Do you know where I can buy a ticket? |

| Nobody gave me the list of the local hotels when I arrived. Could I have one, please? | _____ the list of the local hotels when I arrived. Could I have one, please? |

# unit 2 language B

## 2 Reading: The Dartmoor pony

**a)** Read the text and look up the unknown words in your dictionary.
Then fill in the grid with suitable words from the text.

| activities | pony | attributes |
|---|---|---|
| ride, | | |
| | | |
| | | |
| | | |
| | | |
| | | |

**b)** Read the text again and put in the correct verb forms, active or passive.

Dartmoor ponies are often dark in colour; white markings, if any, are very small. As a hearty moorland breed they are sturdy and similar to a warm blood type. The Dartmoor pony _____was first mentioned_____ (first • mention) in a text from the Middle Ages. Much later, in the 19th century, at the height of tin mining[1] on Dartmoor, the ponies _____(use) for carrying the tin from the mines. When this finished, they _____ (leave) to roam free apart from those that _____ (need) for work around the farms. Until the 1960s quite a number of them _____ (ride) by the warders[2] of Dartmoor prison as they _____ (take) prisoners to and from their work outside.

During the last twenty years special programmes _____ (start) to interest farmers in breeding a true to type Dartmoor pony, robust enough to live outside on Dartmoor all the year round. Here is one example: About ten mares _____ (choose) for breeding and _____ (turn out) in a special place with a Dartmoor stallion. Before that the old stone walls around the fields _____ (must • put up) again and also new fences _____ (build). During the early autumn the mares _____ (collect) and _____ (return) to their owners, the foals _____ (take) to a warmer place. The following year, the programme _____ (continue) with another group of mares and stallions.

[1] ['tɪn ˌmaɪnɪŋ] – Zinnbergbau • [2] ['wɔːdə] – Wärter(in)

## 3 Reading: Letterboxing

**a)** Steffi from Regensburg is on a trip to Dartmoor with Mr Cocker, their language school teacher, who has organised a letterboxing activity for his group. Read the information about letterboxing on Dartmoor.

Dartmoor with its beautiful landscape has been a National Park since 1951. Although it is the home of a lot of typical plants and wildlife, people are allowed to go horseback riding and hiking on the open land. Walking tours are very popular with people of all age groups. They go and look at the great many tors[1] of all shapes and sizes, listen to the ghost stories told about them or they take part in letterboxing, an outdoor activity where people have to find their way across the country with the help of a map and compass[2].

**Rules for letterboxing**
- Don't damage the land.
- Put the box back exactly as you found it.
- Do not take risks.
- Follow the rules.
- Close all gates after use.
- Keep to paths across farmland.
- Leave no rubbish.
- Protect wildlife, wild plants and trees.

[1][tɔː] – typische Felsblöcke in Dartmoor • [2]['kʌmpəs] – Kompass • [3][stæmp] – Stempel

**b)** In the evening Steffi told her host family about her interesting day on Dartmoor.
Write down what she said using the personal passive. Use each of the following words once.

| take | tell | show | give | remind | ask | warn |

1. Today __we were taken__ to Dartmoor and __given__ a brochure about letterboxing.
2. _____ to damage the land and keep to the paths.
3. _____ to follow the rules and put the box back exactly as we had found it.
4. _____ to take any risks.
5. _____ how to close the gates after use.
6. _____ to leave no rubbish and protect wild plants and animals.

# Unit 2 text

## The ghost of St Dominic

### 1 Grammar: What the police had to find out

In 1720, after Captain Parfitt's ship had sunk, the local police had a lot of questions. Ask the questions they had to find answers to. Be careful! Some are in the passive!

1. When exactly _____did the ship sink_____ (the ship • sink)?
2. What _____ (happen • to the crew)?
3. How many _____ (sailors • drown)?
4. If anybody survived, where _____ (they • go)?
5. Where _____ (cargo • take)?
6. Why _____ (the ship • end up • in the little cove)?
7. Who _____ (the fire • make • by)?
8. Who _____ (the wreckers • sell • to • cargo)?

### 2 Writing: The latest news

Mr Saunders, who is almost deaf in one ear, heard people talking in the village shop. Now he's telling his neighbour, Mrs Curtis, the latest news. Correct what he said.

1. There's a young man in the vicar's house who has come from a hospital in France.

2. He's called Jim Nodd and he's spending a few weeks with his uncle, the Reverend Bellows.

3. The reverend is mean to him. He makes him work hard and doesn't feed him well.

4. At first Jack felt lonely because his uncle was always working. So he started to visit the fishing villages along the coast.

5. He's made friends with Rebecca, the housekeeper's wife

6. Sometimes they sit in the church where Rebecca tells him stories from the bible.

## 3 Listening: Booking a ghost tour in London

a) Listen to track 3, then choose the correct answer to the questions. b) Listen again to check your answers.

| | | | |
|---|---|---|---|
| 1. How many people want to go on the ghost tour? | ☐ 10 | ☐ 12 | ☐ 11 |
| 2. How many different tours are there? | ☐ 2 | ☐ 3 | ☐ 4 |
| 3. What is Mrs Oldfield's husband's first name? | ☐ Peter | ☐ Dieter | ☐ Richard |
| 4. When is Halloween? | ☐ October 30th | ☐ October 31st | ☐ November 1st |
| 5. How long does the Halloween tour take? | ☐ one hour | ☐ one and a half hours | ☐ two hours |
| 6. Who is the guide on the ghost tour? | ☐ the men in black | ☐ the woman in black | ☐ a woman in white |
| 7. Mrs Oldfield doesn't want to go on the ghost tour. Why? What do you think? | ☐ She has no money. | ☐ She doesn't play football. | ☐ She's scared. |

## 4 Listening: Cornish ghosts

a) Before you listen to track 4, look at this information:

> What does a dog do when it is pleased? It **wags** its tail.
> A **ghost-hunter** is somebody who goes to old places to look for ghosts.

b) Choose the right answers to complete the sentences. Listen again and check your answers.

1. Margot Murphy talks about ghosts in
   a) Scotland.
   b) Cornwall.
   c) London.

2. The name of the hotel in Boscastle is
   a) the Wellington Hotel.
   b) the Jamaica Inn.
   c) the Napoleon Hotel.

3. The ghost seen by the owner of the Wellington Hotel
   a) jumped from the roof.
   b) went to bed.
   c) walked through the wall.

4. The ghost at the Dolphin Inn in Penzance was
   a) a farmer.
   b) a waiter.
   c) a sailor.

5. The ghost at the Dolphin Inn was sitting
   a) on a chair.
   b) on a wall.
   c) in a boat.

6. The name of the ghost at the house in Duport was
   a) Flo.
   b) Rose.
   c) Nora.

7. The ghost seen by the five-year-old granddaughter was wearing
   a) a black coat.
   b) a blue coat.
   c) a black dress.

8. What does a ghost do when it wants to leave a room?
   a) It opens a cupboard.
   b) It walks through a wall.
   c) It sits on a wall.

twenty-three 23

## 5 Mediation: Piracy[1] today

**a)** Read the following text. Remember that you needn't understand every word.

Piracy has been a problem in the southeast Asian seas for centuries and is becoming an increasing threat[2] to global trade. Nearly two-thirds of all worldwide attacks happen in Asia, most of them taking place in Indonesia's waters and ports.

Sometimes the ships are boarded and hijacked[3] on the high seas, but more often the ships are attacked while they are lying in a port. The targets of an attack are usually parts of the ship's loads, its safe and its crew's valuables. Stealing a whole ship or its complete cargo on the high seas makes only a small part of the reported crimes. Almost all reported acts of piracy are done by armed pirates who threaten[4] and often injure, kidnap, or kill some of the crew.

Today's pirates may be normal fishermen, gangsters, and sometimes even local police. The fact that most attacks happen while a ship is in port or anchored near the coast makes it very probable that some of the police in this region could have something to do with these crimes. Usually the pirates are heavily armed men with military-style weapons; in some cases they were reported to have worn army uniforms and masks.

What might be the reasons for somebody to become a pirate? It is widely known that the economic crisis has made a lot of men lose their jobs so that they can no longer earn enough money to feed their families. Even the police are underpaid, and the military often do not pay their officers and soldiers enough money either which means that a lot of corruption has developed in a number of countries. And for someone working in the police or the army it is easy to get hold of the arms and instruments necessary for hijacking a ship.

[1] ['paɪərəsi] – Piraterie, Seeräuberei • [2] ['θret] – Bedrohung • [3] ['haɪdʒæk] – kapern • [4] ['θretn] – bedrohen

**b)** This is part of a report that students from different countries have just been given at their language school. Florian didn't listen carefully so he'll have to ask his neighbour what exactly the report was about. He has collected his questions in German. Write the dialogue between Florian and Mike. The verbs may be active or passive.

1. Ist Seeräuberei ein neues Problem in Südostasien?
2. Warum schreiben die Zeitungen häufig darüber?
3. Wo werden die Schiffe überfallen?
4. Was wird normalerweise gestohlen?
5. Werden Menschen bei Überfällen verletzt?
6. Wer sind die Piraten?
7. Warum wird jemand zum Pirat?
8. Woher bekommen die Piraten moderne Waffen?

*Florian:* <u>Is piracy a new problem in southeast Asia?</u>

*Mike:* No, not really, it has been a problem _____

*Florian:* _____

*Mike:* Well, it _____ a bigger and bigger risk on the seas.

*Florian:* _____

*Mike:* Sometimes the ships are _____ on the high seas, but quite often it happens in the ports, too.

*Florian:* _____

*Mike:* The pirates are mostly interested in _____

Very rarely whole ships or cargoes _____

*Florian:* _____

*Mike:* Yes, they are. Very often the crew are _____ or even _____

*Florian:* _____

*Mike:* Actually, all sorts of people can _____ pirates. They may be _____ _____ _____ or even the local police, which is highly probable because most attacks _____ in the ports.

*Florian:* _____

*Mike:* There are very many poor people in this region and a lot of men have families who have to _____. What can they do when they have no work? Even the police and the soldiers _____ _____

*Florian:* _____ _____

*Mike:* There is quite a lot of corruption in these countries, you know. So weapons might _____ from soldiers or the police, if they themselves do not take part in the crimes anyway.

## On the southwestern coast

**let's check**

### 1 Grammar: The Magic¹ Wizzix

Mr Laziman believes in everything that is modern, so he bought a Magic Wizzix on the Internet some weeks ago. But after four weeks he was really annoyed. Mr Laziman talked to his neighbour Mrs Bisibee.

**A fantastic cleaner!**

Your rooms have never been so clean!
**Cleans the air:** Your rooms won't smell of dogs anymore. **Moves around** easily! Magic Wizzix works wonders! Magic Wizzix's **magic broom²** cleans walls and ceilings. Just mount³ the broom and push. Magic Wizzix does all you want by itself. It's just magic!

**Excellent service!** Any problem? Call us or write an e-mail, we'll be there to help you at once.

"I was really happy to have my new Magic Wizzix, but then things began to go wrong. I'm sure, I did everything just as ___I was told___ (tell). _____ **(promise)** that it would move around the room easily, but then when I left it to work alone it bumped into my television and broke it. _____ **(tell)** that it can remove the smell

¹['mædʒɪk] – magisch • ²[bruːm] – Besen • ³[maʊnt] – aufbauen; aufsteigen

of dogs. Could I borrow your dog to test if it's true? _____ (inform) that I could mount its broom and play a game of Quidditch[4]. So I opened the window, stood on the kitchen table and climbed onto the broom. But when I switched my Wizzix on, it didn't take me up into the air. Instead I fell from the table and hurt my foot. There was a big spot[5] on my wall in the living room, you know. I _____ (advise) by my son not to mount the broom again to clean the wall. Maybe I'll fall off again. I have already written an e-mail to the company, but _____ (not give) an answer yet. Look here, Mrs Bisibee, _____ (offer) help at any time of the day. But when I ring this number, it's always engaged. Can't you help me?"

[4] a ride on a broom in Harry Potter • [5] [spɔt] – Fleck

## 2 Grammar: Helpful Mrs Bisibee

Of course, Mrs Bisibee was able to help her neighbour. She had been waiting for her chance to help and didn't stop talking when Mr Laziman asked her for help. Use conditional sentences.

"Of course, I'll help you, Mr Laziman. If I'd read about the Magic Wizzix, I __wouldn't__ __have trusted__ (not trust) those promises. If you _____ (buy) something on the Internet, you never know whether you can give it back. If I _____ (be) you, I _____ (write) a letter to the company and complain. But wouldn't it be a good idea, if you _____ (show) me your Wizzix first. I _____ (can try) and help, if you let me in. … Oh dear, is that the spot you wanted to clean? If you really _____ (want) the wall to be clean again, you must … Oh, actually, I can clean it for you, if you _____ (make) us a nice cup of tea. Tell me, Mr Laziman, do you really believe in magic? If somebody else had told me your story, I _____ (not believe) it. Never mind, if you _____ (not have got) any tea at home, come over to my place. You know, if you _____ (be) interested in Quidditch, we could go to the cinema together. We could watch the new Harry Potter film, if you _____ (like). I _____ (be) very pleased if you'd spend the evening with me. Come on, if we _____ (not hurry) up, we'll be late for the film."

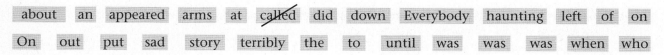

## 1 Reading: A legend from Devon

Complete the text with these words as shown in line 1.

about an appeared arms at ~~called~~ did down Everybody haunting left of on
On out put sad story terribly the to until was was was when who

Long ago, back in the 17th century, a young woman | Anne Taylor lived near a little Exmoor town. As with many legends, her is about two men loved the same woman. One of them, John Howard, was very jealous, and it was him who she in the end. Of course he was. Day after day he thought his lost love and he began to hate Anne. At last the day came Anne and the new man in her life decided to get married. It did not take long John got the news, too.

called

He felt hurt and sank into a deep silence. On day of their wedding[1] her future husband stood waiting at the altar with a loving smile his face. After the ceremony husband and wife walked the church and stepped outside. Suddenly a loud bang heard. For a moment it was as if time had stood still, nobody moved and nobody spoke. looked in shock the body of Anne Taylor. Her white dress covered in the blood which slowly came of a small hole over her heart. Her husband got on his knees beside her and took her small lifeless body in his with tears running down his face. It was as if he trying to put her to sleep.

Legend does not say what happened to Anne's killer, but if there is any truth in event of 1965, her soul is still the place. In that year a young woman was going get married in the same church. the morning of the wedding a young woman wearing a 17th century wedding dress to a guest just outside his room. Luckily the bride[2] of 1965 not take this to be a bad sign and went ahead with the wedding. It is said that she her bridal bouquet[3] on the grave Anne Taylor as a symbol of respect.

1['wedɪŋ] – Hochzeit • 2[braɪd] – Braut • 3[ˌbraɪdl bʊ'keɪ] – Brautstrauß

# Young people in Scotland

## 1 Mixed bag: Three teenagers

While Florian was travelling through Scotland with his parents, he met three very different teenagers. Use the following words to connect the sentences.

| however | which | in order to | although | whose | when | because | apart from | like | as |
| since | who | and | also | instead of | although | in fact | which | where | who |

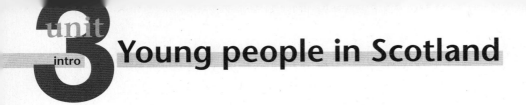

**Amir**, _____ parents own a corner shop in Glasgow, is a great Celtic fan. _____ he has to work hard for school, he sometimes helps in the shop _____ he wants to earn some money. He needs it for football tickets and _____ for another expensive hobby: CDs and concerts. _____ there are so many rock groups in Glasgow, he sometimes can't decide _____ concert to go to. But in the end he always finds a friend _____ wants to go with him and then they decide together.

**Emma**, _____ he met at the bed and breakfast place _____ they spent their first night in the Highlands, is a totally different person. _____ she lives quite a long way from her school, _____ right at the southern end of Loch Ness, she is picked up by a bus every morning _____ takes her to school. _____ there is not much to do in her part of Scotland, she doesn't feel bored. _____ her friend Hazel she speaks with a strong Scottish accent.

**Mark**, _____, doesn't have a Scottish accent, as he is from England _____ has lived in Scotland for only a year. They moved to Aberdeen _____ his father was given a job on an oil rig. _____ some typically Scottish traditions, Mark doesn't find life in Scotland so very different. _____ going to pop concerts, some people here like to go to a ceilidh from time to time _____ enjoy dancing, singing and listening to stories.

## 2 Vocabulary: Countries and their people

| country | people | nationality |
|---|---|---|
| Spain | Spaniard, the Spanish (pl.) | Spanish |
| Britain | | |
| England | | |
| Scotland | | |
| Ireland | | |
| France | | |

**28** twenty-eight

# Please, Dad!

## 1 Speaking: Dialogues

Complete the dialogues with phrases from the box. Learn the sentences by heart. They contain some important phrases with the indefinite article.

> 24 hours a day • in a hurry • quite a long way •
> for a change • a pity • six days a week •
> rather an interesting new game •
> quarter of an hour ago • an American • a headache •
> two and a half hours • 55p a piece • 90p a kilo •
> a software designer • three times a week • a silly idea

**1.** *Mrs McArthur:* Brian's mother? She's _____ in Edinburgh.

*Mrs McDonald:* Do you think she has time for a cup of tea?

*Mrs McArthur:* I'm not sure. She's _____ because she has to travel to her firm _____

*Mrs McDonald:* I see. That's _____ . Is she Scottish?

*Mrs McArthur:* No, I think she's _____ , but her husband is Scottish.


**2.** *Mike:* Hi Brian. Would you like to come out and play football with us?

*Brian:* No, sorry. I'm ill. I've got _____

*Mike:* What _____ ! Let's play cards _____
I know _____

*Brian:* _____
We're not babies!


**3.** *Mr Wilson:* Could I talk to your dad, please?

*David:* Sorry, he left _____

*Mr Wilson:* OK. I'll call again in _____ !


**4.** *Customer:* When do you close for the night?

*Owner:* We're open _____

*Customer:* Are you open every day?

*Owner:* No, only _____ . We're closed on Mondays.

*Customer:* How much are the apples?

*Owner:* They're _____

*Customer:* And that chocolate cake?

*Owner:* Oh, that's _____

## 2 Grammar: Florian's letter

Put a tick (✔) in the box when the *definite article* is needed.

Dear Patrick,
We almost missed ✔ B&B, when we drove up from ☐ Loch Ness last night. ☐ Campbells live in such a sweet little house. Mrs Campbell gave us a warm welcome and offered us a cup of ☐ tea. She didn't invite us for ☐ tea though because they only do ☐ bed and breakfast. Oh boy, ☐ breakfast this morning, I'll never forget it. To start with, we had ☐ porridge, then ☐ bacon and ☐ eggs with ☐ sausages, ☐ baked beans and ☐ fried tomatoes. Mrs Campbell made us one of her specialities: ☐ fried bread, just like her children like it. You know, she had baked ☐ bread herself. Of course, there was ☐ orange juice and ☐ tea or ☐ coffee. I actually had ☐ tea, because I didn't like ☐ juice. It was a bit sweet. When we got up from ☐ table, we were so full that we decided not to take ☐ car. We really needed to go for a long walk along ☐ loch. Don't laugh but I took my camera, ☐ new digital one, just in case I saw ☐ Nessie. Unfortunately we didn't, although I had ☐ impression that I saw a funny shape in ☐ mist in ☐ distance. It must be hard for ☐ poor old Nessie. All ☐ tourists that come here want to take ☐ photos of her. Emma, ☐ Campbells' daughter promised to show me the place from where she had once seen ☐ monster.
So much for today,
Florian

## 3 C-test: Hogmanay

Complete the text. Each blank (☐) stands for one letter.

New Year's Eve, 31 De☐☐☐☐☐☐☐, is traditionally the most imp☐☐☐☐☐☐☐ day in the Highlands, even more important th☐☐ Christmas. Today people cel☐☐☐☐☐☐☐ with th☐☐☐ friends; they dance, sing, eat and drink. In the past, Hogmanay, the last day of the year, w☐☐ connected w☐☐☐ a lot of magical rituals¹ to drive out evil powers. So it is no sur☐☐☐☐☐ that a lot of dif☐☐☐☐☐☐☐ Hogmanay customs ex☐☐☐☐☐☐ all over Scotland. Usually young boys went round the houses, lou☐☐☐ singing "Hogmanay Poems". The boys took p☐☐☐ in special rituals called "Hogmanay Lads²". They were dre☐☐☐☐ in cow skins; one of them cov☐☐☐☐ with the skin of a bull with the horns and the hooves still on. They made a terrible no☐☐☐ singing and beating the skins and the walls of the ho☐☐☐☐☐ with sticks. They were inv☐☐☐☐ into the houses and offered fo☐☐ and drink. In some parts of Sc☐☐☐☐☐☐ the man of the house held the skin in the fire and every member of the fa☐☐☐☐ had to smell the stinking sm☐☐☐ which was beli☐☐☐☐ to clean the house from anything evil and br☐☐☐ health to the family for the next twelve mo☐☐☐☐☐. The ho☐☐☐☐ were decorated with holly³ in order to k☐☐☐ out bad fairies; and juniper⁴ was burnt in front of the cattle to pro☐☐☐☐ them. Cheese was also believed to h☐☐☐ magical powers. A piece of cheese with a h☐☐☐ in it was thought to be esp☐☐☐☐☐☐☐ valuable because if a per☐☐☐ got lost in the mi☐☐ in the hills and he lo☐☐☐☐ through the hole, he w☐☐☐☐ immediately know where he was.

¹['rɪtjuəl] – Ritual, Ritus • ²[læd] – *Scottish:* boy • ³['hɒli] – Stechpalme • ⁴['dʒuːnɪpə] – Wachholder

# It makes me so angry!

language B

## 1 Mediation: The test

Iris is furious. She was given a very bad mark for her geography test. Outside the classroom she meets her Scottish exchange partner Liz and her friends. What would their conversation be like in English? Use the following expressions, but don't translate word by word.

go on about something[1] • to stand •
what's it all about? • to mark a test • all over •
to be mean • honestly • to join • to enjoy

*Liz:* Was hat dich so wütend gemacht?

*Iris:* Ich hasse sie. Sie hat stundenlang über die Benachteiligten, die Armen, die Blinden und Kranken geredet, über all jene Menschen und Krankheiten in Afrika. Ich kann es nicht mehr ertragen. Irgendwann ist bei jedem einmal die Schmerzgrenze erreicht.

*Liz:* Es ist ja in Ordnung mal Dampf abzulassen. Aber sag mal, worum geht's eigentlich?

*Iris:* Schau her, wie sie meinen Test benotet hat. Die einzige Benachteiligte bin ich. Ich habe so viel gelernt letztes Wochenende. Zwei Stunden lang nach Tinas Geburtstagsparty, bis ich eingeschlafen bin.

*Liz:* Es ist ja überall rot. Und du hast ja nur die Hälfte der Fragen beantwortet.

*Iris:* Sie hat uns nicht genug Zeit gegeben. Sie ist so gemein. Und Julia hat kürzlich mit angehört, wie sie sich über unsere Klasse beschwert hat. Sie wollte sich bloß rächen.

*Liz:* Aber ehrlich, du kannst sie doch nicht verantwortlich machen. Es ist doch nicht ihre Schuld, dass du nach der Party zu müde warst, um zu lernen. Ich hoffe, du warst zu ihr nicht unverschämt. Los, gehen wir zu den andern und machen wir uns einen schönen Nachmittag.

*Liz:* _____
*Iris:* _____

[1] stundenlang über etwas reden

## 2 Vocabulary: Crossword puzzle

**Across →**
1. Ghosts do it.
6. A line of people who are waiting.
7. To divide, to pull things apart.
8. To say it's somebody's fault.
10. A subject or problem that's often discussed.
11. A place for children without parents.
12. An important thing we mustn't waste.

**Down ↓**
2. To believe something is true but not be quite sure.
3. A … person likes to give things to others.
4. A kind of metal used for making bridges, cars, etc.
5. Some people believe that if you … a place, bad luck will come to it.
9. A document that allows you to do something.

## 3 Mediation: Singular or plural?

Find the correct translation.

1. Vorsicht! Die Treppe ist sehr steil.

_____

2. Ich kann meine Brille nicht finden. Wo habe ich sie hingelegt?

_____

3. Sind die Nachrichten an? – Gut. Schauen wir sie an.

_____

4. Eure neuen Möbel sehen wirklich schön aus. Wo habt ihr sie gekauft?

_____

5. Ich brauche einen Rat.

_____

6. Die Polizei sucht den Dieb.

_____

7. Das Vieh wird bald verkauft werden.

_____

8. Die USA sind ein sehr interessantes Land.

_____

**32** thirty-two

## 4 Speaking: At the youth hostel

At the end of their school trip to Stonehaven near Aberdeen Amir's class have to tidy their rooms at the youth hostel. Put in the correct possessive pronouns.

*Amir:* Is that your sock, Angus?

*Angus:* No, it isn't _____. Ask Brian, perhaps it's _____ .

*Colin:* Hey, Chris, this comic isn't _____ , is it? Did Fiona leave it in our room?

*Chris:* No, it isn't _____ and it isn't _____ , either. I gave _____ to Coleen when she looked in this morning. Maybe it's one of Anne's, she has quite a lot of them.

*Mr Adams:* Amir, Chris, have you got your bags ready?

*Amir:* Yes, Mr Adams, _____ are packed, but Trevor and Bob haven't finished packing. They can't bring _____ down yet.

*Mr Adams:* When all your rooms are tidy, there'll be ice cream for everybody!

*Everybody:* Great, Mr Adams, that's a fantastic idea of _____ .

## 5 Vocabulary: *Do* or *make*?

Put in phrases with 'do' or 'make'. Think about the tenses.

I'm trying to _____ my best. Don't _____ fun of me!

Oh boy, the sun _____ me good! We _____ the most of our holiday, aren't we?

And who _____ the cooking?

I _____ it most of the time, but we share the housework. Dad _____ the shopping, and luckily the machine _____ the washing up.

… and finally we _____ our way to the top of the mountain.

Did you _____ friends with the other hikers?

No, not really, but it was good to go down together in the mist.

My new car _____ 160 mph. It's a pity I can't drive it so fast on our highways.

This drink is _____ of ice tea, orange juice and …

Sorry, I've no time. Mum _____ me tidy my room and I haven't _____ my homework yet.

My car was broken into and to _____ matters worse, the thieves got my credit card, too.

Let me help you _____ the puzzle.

thirty-three 33

language B

## 6 Reading: A Scotland quiz

Test what you know about Scotland. Use your dictionary for words you don't know. The letters give you the name of a famous Scottish football team:

☐☐☐☐☐☐☐ ☐☐☐☐☐☐☐
1. 2. 3. 4. 5. 6. 7.   8. 9. 10. 11. 12. 13. 14.

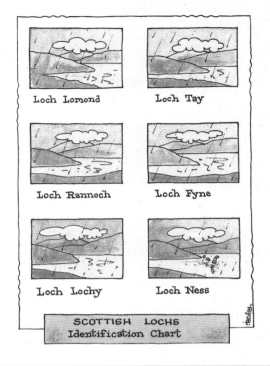

SCOTTISH LOCHS Identification Chart

1. **shortbread**
   - B) like a French baguette only shorter
   - G) a Scottish biscuit
   - E) a short piece of wood used for building bridges in Scotland

2. **Highlander**
   - O) a special kind of whisky
   - I) a worker on one of the huge oil-rigs
   - L) a person living in the Scottish mountains

3. **Nessie**
   - A) a monster
   - S) Lassie's sister
   - F) a character in a Scottish family series

4. **loch**
   - V) a cave smugglers use for stolen goods
   - S) that's what the Scots call their lakes
   - B) a prison in Edinburgh

5. **Ben**
   - G) the Scottish word for 'mountain'
   - U) a clock tower in Glasgow
   - R) the Scottish form of 'Benjamin'

6. **thistle**
   - A) what Scottish boys do when they see a pretty girl
   - O) (a plant) Scottish symbol on British pound coins
   - F) what Scottish boys call their sisters

7. **porridge**
   - C) a vegetable with long green leaves
   - W) what Scots often eat for breakfast
   - T) the shape of the Scottish hills against the sunset

8. **haggis**
   - A) a Scottish mountain animal with two short legs and two longer ones
   - L) a Scottish square dance
   - R) a Scottish meat dish

9. **lassie**
   - A) Scottish word for a girl
   - H) a Scottish non-alcoholic drink
   - M) a kind of dog from the Highlands

10. **hogmanay**
    - U) a man who looks after pigs on a Scottish farm
    - P) an animal living in the Highlands
    - N) the 31st December

11. **kilt**
    - Q) the past participle of 'to kill'
    - G) Scottish men wear them sometimes
    - S) a Scottish girl's miniskirt

12. **firth**
    - U) the title of the Scottish Prime Minister
    - A) the name of a forest tree in Scotland
    - E) a bay, part of the sea in Scotland

13. **tartan**
    - R) the colours and pattern of a Scottish family
    - J) the football shirt worn by Celtic Glasgow
    - F) a Scottish cake

14. **Hebrides**
    - D) a Scottish boy group
    - S) a group of islands off the Scottish west coast
    - I) certain stars in Scottish winter skies

# The kiss

## 1 Vocabulary: Crossword puzzle

**Across →**
2. A place that is too full of people or things is …
6. A subject in which you learn how to plan and design buildings.
8. A very wide road on which cars can go fast.
10. You cannot get onto a plane … you show your boarding pass.
11. If you … something, you get it from a person that has died and left it to you.
12. A subject or problem that is important and often discussed.

**Down ↓**
1. People use them to light a fire, a candle or a cigarette.
3. If you think that something may not be true, you … it.
4. All the people who live in a place are its …
5. People who like to give things to others, e.g. to the poor or to charities, are very …
6. If you … something, you think it is true although you do not really know.
7. A traditional kind of food that is eaten for breakfast, e.g. in Scotland and in Scandinavian countries.
9. If something is …, it is the only one of its kind.

## 2 Grammar: Adjectives as nouns

Write down the missing English or German expression.

_____ : die Arbeitslosen          _____ : die Lebenden

a Welsh lady : _____          _____ und die Toten

_____ : einige Reiche          a sick person : _____

the rich : _____          _____ : ein Franzose

and the poor _____          a blind man : _____

_____ : ein Toter          _____ : die Blinden

three Scotsmen : _____          a disadvantaged girl : _____

_____ : die Engländer          _____ : die Obdachlosen

a group of : _____          the needy : _____

disabled people _____          _____ das Gute daran

_____ : der Kleine          _____

## 3 Vocabulary: Dictionary work

The following expressions all have to do with 'fire'. Look up the words you don't know in your dictionary. Write down the English and German expressions.

1. fire engine    2. _____    3. _____    4. _____

   Feuerwehrauto

5. _____    6. _____    7. _____    8. _____

9. _____    10. _____    11. _____    12. _____

## 4 Listening: A short history of Scottish tartan

**5** Listen to the interview in track 5. Then write complete sentences like those in the listening text using the clues and starting with the words that are given.

1. Mary said that tartan is very popular all over the world.
   **Clues: tartan – popular – world**

2. The Celts _____

   **Clues: call themselves – 'Scoti' – come – Ireland – settle – Scotland – 5th century**

3. The Scoti _____
   **Clues: use – tartan clothes – show – position – family**

4. From the 12th century on, _____

   **Clues: people – Lowlands – begin to learn – language – north of England**

5. The climate in Scotland is _____

   **Clues: cold and wet – need – dress – warm clothes**

6. After 1746 _____

   **Clues: Scottish soldiers – lowland Scots – women – wear – the tartan**

**36** thirty-six

## 5 Mixed bag: Error-spotting

Read the sentences about the story 'The kiss'. In one of the four words from each sentence there is a mistake. Mark the wrong word with ✗ and write the correct one on the line below.

1. Chris has always been the odd one out because his face is lopsided and his face has a strange colour and his upper lip is hardly visible.

   ▪ odd one   ✗ has   ▪ upper   ▪ hardly
   _____is_____

2. Chris's older sister played with matches when he was three and his cart caught fire with Chris sitting in it.

   ▪ Chris's   ▪ matches   ▪ cart   ▪ sitting
   _____

3. Mr Conway, their Science teacher, chose Chris for an experience and when he struck a match something caught fire.

   ▪ chose   ▪ experience   ▪ struck   ▪ caught
   _____

4. Chris admitted that he was only chosen as an assistant for the experiment because he had given a very good mark for his last assignment.

   ▪ admitted   ▪ had got   ▪ had given
   ▪ assignment _____

5. Chris's heart was beating fast when Karl held a burning match in front of his face and said he will burn off his eyelashes with it.

   ▪ heart   ▪ fast   ▪ will   ▪ burn off
   _____

6. Spike and Karl stopped terrifying Chris with the burning match because Chris said he'd do anything. So Spike meant that they had got a result.

   ▪ terrifying   ▪ to do   ▪ meant   ▪ result
   _____

7. The first few times Chris didn't steel from shops. He took cigarettes from his mum's bag, and a bottle of whisky from the drinks cupboard. Later Chris stole things from Mr Patel's corner shop.

   ▪ mum's   ▪ steel   ▪ things   ▪ Mr Patel's
   _____

8. Chris did not want to appear a coward in front of Shelby. And although he felt like a wimp he wanted Shelby to admire him. But when he saw that Karl had inspired the fireworks …

   ▪ coward   ▪ wimp   ▪ admire   ▪ inspired
   _____

9. Chris noticed that Shelby's eyes were wide of horror and he thought that it was because his face was so close to hers. Shelby shouted, pushed Chris to one side and reached for the firework.

   ▪ noticed   ▪ wide of   ▪ close to
   ▪ reached for _____

## 6 Listening: Museums in Edinburgh

a) Listen to track 6. Mr Stuart talks about seven museums. Can you match their names with what you can see in them? b) Listen again to check your answers.

The Museum of Scotland — Children's toys and games
The Museum of Scottish Life — The history of the Scottish people
The Concorde Museum — Science and space travel
The Royal Museum — The fastest passenger plane
Museum of Costume — Art objects
Interactive Science and Technology Gallery — Clothes
The Museum of Childhood — Farm animals

# Young people in Scotland

## let's check

### 1 Mediation: In English, please

1. Können Sie mir bitte Feuer geben?
2. Machen wir doch ein Lagerfeuer!
3. Wer hat den Feueralarm ausgelöst?
4. Sein Onkel ist schon seit 20 Jahren Feuerwehrmann.
5. Bei den Thomsons brennt ein Feuer (im Kamin).
6. Sie schafften es nicht den Waldbrand zu löschen.
7. Hast du schon einmal ein richtiges Feuerwerk gesehen?
8. Sei vorsichtig, dass deine Bluse nicht Feuer fängt!
9. Irgendjemand hat den Schuppen unserer Nachbarn in Brand gesteckt.

### 2 Grammar: Singular and plural words

Fill in the correct English expressions.

1. For _____ (**weitere Auskünfte**) please apply to the manager.

2. He gave me several _____ (**gute Ratschläge**) on how to repair my computer, but the best _____ (**Ratschlag • war**) to buy a new one.

3. Could you lend me _____ (**deine Jeans**), please? – No, I'm sorry, I want to wear _____ (**sie**) myself. Why don't you wear your own _____ (**Hose**)?

4. A lot of people think _____ (**Mathematik • ist**) a very difficult subject.

5. Look, my mother has bought _____ (**eine Sonnenbrille**) for our holiday.

6. "No news _____ (**to be**) good news," Grandpa Jones used to say when he didn't get any mail.

7. Oh, Gary, just look at _____ (**diese Möbel**)! _____ (**Sind sie nicht**) wonderful? – Yes, of course, but 3,000 pounds _____ (**to be**) a lot of money!

**38** thirty-eight

# Focus on the New World

## 1 Vocabulary: The alphabet competition

You can play the alphabet game with a friend as it is described on page 142 in your text book. Here is another version. Fill in the words defined on the right.

| | | |
|---|---|---|
| a | _as best we can_ | • If we try to do something very, very well, we do it … |
| b | _____ | • a nicely cut flat piece of wood (You can build a cabin with it.) |
| c | _____ | • hard, round pieces of money ➔ |
| d | _____ | • another word for illness |
| e | _____ | • a change or event that is the result of something |
| f | _____ | • a person that is strange, because of his or her looks or opinions |
| g | _____ | • an animal that is trained to help blind people to find their way |
| h | _____ | • People who do not have enough time are in a … |
| i | _____ | • complete freedom from others ➔ |
| j | _____ | • the people who live in Japan |
| k | _____ | • a brave and noble person of the Middle Ages |
| l | _____ | • you do this when you hear a good joke |
| m | _____ | • adjective of 'medicine' |
| n | _____ | • to say 'yes' by moving your head up and down |
| o | _____ | • something that lasts for a very long time or forever |
| p | _____ | • religious group of the 17th century ➔ |
| q | _____ | • They settled in Pennsylvania. ➔ |
| r | _____ | • noun of 'religious' |
| s | _____ | • a building used to keep goods in |
| t | _____ | • to exchange, buy or sell goods |
| u | _____ | • opposite of 'beautiful' |
| v | _____ | • A priest is to a Catholic what a … is to a Protestant. |
| w | _____ | • made from wood |
| x | _____ | • a shorter way of writing 'Christmas' in English |
| y | _____ | • you say this when something tastes delicious |
| z | _____ | • Some clothes do not have buttons, they have … |

# Unit 4 intro: New England

## 1 Reading: The Pilgrims as people

In each line one word is missing. Complete the text – as shown in line 1 – with the words in the box.

> through • difficulties • themselves • country • familiar • shared • ~~surrounded~~ • heroes • emigrating • in • example • the • were • escape • communities • without • who • of

**The Pilgrims as people: Understanding the Plymouth colonists**

The people we know as the Pilgrims have become with so many legends
                        surrounded
that we almost forget that they were real people. In spite of great, they
bravely made the famous 1620 voyage[1] and founded first New England
colony, but they were still ordinary English men and women, not super.
If we really want to understand them, we must try to look behind the
legends and see them as they saw.

They were English people who wanted to the religious controversies[2] and
economic problems of their time by to America. Many of the Pilgrims
were Puritans. They believed that membership in the Church England was
against the rules in the bible, and that they had to break away and form
independent Christian which were truer to God. At a time when Church
and State one, such an act was against the law and the Puritans had to leave
their mother.

As English people, the Pilgrims also a living culture. They were not people
just like ourselves but dressed in funny clothes, or a primitive folk our
technology, but a strong and courageous[3] people embodied the best
elements of their exciting society. They brought their own culture to the
New World and tried to set a good of English society on the edge of an alien
continent. They were not pioneers making a trail the wilderness to the
future. They were English men and women with their customs, doing their
best to continue[4] the lives they knew back home spite of the unfamiliar
surroundings.

[1][vɔɪdʒ] – Schiffsreise • [2][ˈkɒntrəvɜːsi] – Auseinandersetzung • [3][kəˈreɪdʒəs] – mutig • [4][kənˈtɪnjuː] – weitermachen

# An e-mail from Susie

language A — unit 4

## 1 Vocabulary: Opposites

wealthy ↔ _poor_

_____ ↔ empty

interior ↔ _____

_____ ↔ software

to get married ↔ _____

_____ ↔ dependent

unspectacular ↔ _____

to decrease ↔ _____

_____ ↔ tension

advantage ↔ _____

_____ ↔ hero

beautiful ↔ _____

_____ ↔ health

boring ↔ _____

## 2 Writing: Explaining words

Explain the **marked** words with a complete sentence. Use one expression from the box in each sentence.

> may be • might be • perhaps • probably • certainly • possibly • most likely

1. a **useless** tin opener
(*wahrscheinlich*)

1. That probably is a tin opener _____

2. an **enjoyable** evening
(*kann sein*)

3. an **inexperienced** leader
(*vielleicht*)

4. a **spectacular** video clip
(*könnte sein*)

5. an **unforgettable** journey
(*höchstwahrscheinlich*)

6. an **eventful** summer holiday
(*sicherlich*)

7. an **unsinkable** ferry
(*möglicherweise*)

### language A

### 3 Speaking: Bits of conversations

Complete what these people say – with suitable gerunds and prepositions. Use these verbs:

do    spend    live    travel    speak    wait    learn    hike    jog

1. Are you looking forward _____ your holiday in the south of France?

2. Barbara loves all sports apart _____ .

3. My brother is interested _____ to ride a motor-bike. Can you teach him?

4. Have you ever thought _____ in the mountains for a few days? It's good exercise.

5. Sorry, I'm not used _____ such hard work. I'm only a student after all.

6. What _____ for the next bus? It's much cheaper than taking a taxi.

7. Most young Europeans are keen _____ to other countries even if they are not so good _____ the language.

8. Has your sister got used _____ so far away from home or is she still homesick[1]?

[1] ['həʊmsɪk] – Heimweh haben

### language B

## The 1627 Pilgrim Village

### 1 Speaking: Going on vacation in New England

Sarah and Gary Higgins were talking about their next holiday. Write down what they said and decide whether to use a gerund (plus preposition) or an infinitive.

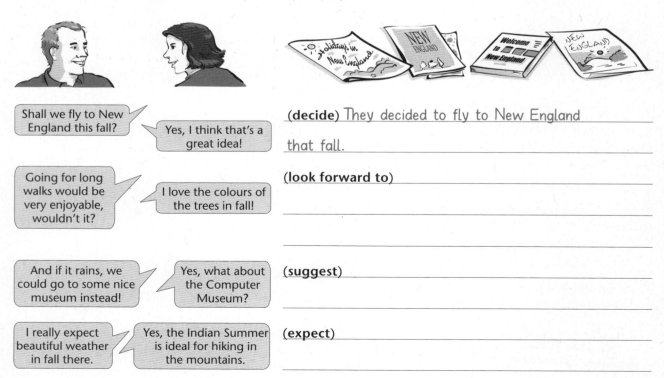

(decide) They decided to fly to New England that fall.

(look forward to) _____

(suggest) _____

(expect) _____

| | | |
|---|---|---|
| Where should we stay then? | Hotels are rather expensive in that area, aren't they? | (complain) _____ |
| Maybe we could stay on one of those farms in Vermont. | Yes, with a wonderful view of the rolling hills. | (think) _____ |
| Do you think we could also go to Cape Cod? | I'm not quite sure if we'll have time enough to do that. | (not know) _____ |
| It's so difficult to book a room on the Internet. | Why don't you just give them a call, Gary? | (want) _____ |
| | | (be worth) _____ |
| We could have some lobster in some fishing port on the coast. | But they are terribly expensive even there! | |

## 2 Mediation: A teacher's thoughts after a visit to the Pilgrim Village

Say it in English by using gerund constructions.

1. Es hat sich wirklich gelohnt, die Plymouth Colony mit meinen Schülern zu besuchen.

   <u>It was really worth</u>

2. Sie waren sehr daran interessiert, das Leben der frühen Siedler kennen zu lernen.

   _____

3. Nur einer von ihnen beschwerte sich darüber, dass er keine Gelegenheit hatte, sich mit einem der Rollenspieler zu unterhalten.

   _____
   _____

4. Allerdings mochten einige die Vorstellung nicht, über ihren Ausflug ein Referat halten zu müssen.

   _____
   _____

5. Was haltet ihr davon, zu versuchen in der Plymouth Colony einen Ferienjob zu bekommen?

   _____
   _____

## 3 Writing: The Thompsons at Hobbamock's Homesite

Connect the sentences by using gerunds together with the words on the right.

> instead of • without • in spite of • apart from • by

1. When the Thompsons wanted to go into the museum shop, it was too crowded with people. So they went to Hobbamock's Homesite.

   _Instead of going_ _____

2. Although they visited Hobbamock's Homesite, they didn't have a chance to talk to one of the Native Americans there.

3. The Thompsons did just about everything during their stay there, but they didn't taste any of the food made by the Native Americans.

4. In the end they learned a lot about the history of the early settlers. They read an excellent guide book about them.

## 4 Grammar: Infinitive or gerund?

W ☐ ☐ ☐ ☐ ☐ ☐ ☐
1. 2. 3. 4. 5. 6. 7. 8.

Draw a circle around the letter next to the correct verb forms and write the letters in the boxes above. If your answers are right, you'll get the name of one of the Pilgrims' religious leaders. His name was John …

1. David has been looking forward **(visit)** the Pilgrim Village with his classmates all week.
   - **(w)** to visiting
   - **x** to visit
   - **y** visiting

2. He simply couldn't imagine **(cross)** the Atlantic in a sailing ship like that?
   - **g** to cross
   - **h** at crossing
   - **i** crossing

3. Nobody stopped **(talk)**. It was impossible for their teacher **(hear)** the guide's explanations.
   - **l** to talk – to hear
   - **m** in order to talk – to hear
   - **n** talking – to hear

4. "What do you think **(have)** a break before **(go)** to Hobbamock's Homesite?" Mr Hooker asked.
   - **r** having – going
   - **s** about having – to go
   - **t** of having – going

5. "Are you keen **(eat)** some of their food? Or would you prefer **(have)** your sandwiches?"
   - **g** on eating – having
   - **h** on eating – to have
   - **i** to eat – to have

6. Some of the role players find it hard to get used **(speak)** this 17th century English dialect.
   - **r** to speaking
   - **s** to speak
   - **t** speaking

7. It was fascinating **(watch)** the women at work. They were so clever **(handle)** the enormous pots.
   - **m** to watch – to handle
   - **n** watching – handling
   - **o** to watch – at handling

8. In spite **(have)** to walk a lot, most of the students thought it was really worth **(come)** here.
   - **p** of having – coming
   - **q** to have – to come
   - **r** of having – to come

# The ransom

## 1 Vocabulary: Word families

| noun | adjective | noun | adjective |
|---|---|---|---|
| | important | | valuable |
| wood | | poison | |
| | independent | | fascinating |
| fury | | enjoyment | |
| | depressed | | electric |
| religion | | generosity | |
| | special | | spectacular |
| divorce | | medicine | |

Now use suitable nouns or adjectives from the lists to complete these sentences.

1. Did you hear that a _____ painting has been stolen from the National Gallery?
2. When the USA became _____ in 1776, the British started a war against them.
3. In the past people used _____ spoons and forks, because metal was expensive.
4. Everybody knows about the _____ of London as the capital of Britain.
5. Sometimes a _____ is the only answer to the problems of married couples.
6. The Baxters like giving money to the poor. They are well-known for their _____ .
7. The _____ Mr Gregg gets out of playing golf is unbelievable. He simply loves it.

## 2 Mediation: Prepositions

Express these phrases in English but think about the prepositions.

1. Ab / Auf nach Massachusetts!
2. Gehen wir doch in die Innenstadt!
3. Da ist ein Flugzeug am Himmel.
4. Er ist gut im Kochen, aber schlecht im Feuer machen.
5. Das ist eine CD von den Red Hot Chili Peppers.
6. Lassen Sie mich bitte hier aussteigen!
7. Die Pilger übergaben ein wichtiges Dokument.

8. Cambridge liegt direkt neben Boston. _____
9. Susie kann heute nicht in die Schule gehen. _____
10. Das hat er absichtlich gemacht! _____
11. Warum ist er auf der Flucht? _____
12. Können Sie das Ergebnis der Ermittlungen zusammenfassen? _____
13. Kate ist gern unterwegs. _____
14. Meiner Meinung nach ist der Herbst die beste Jahreszeit zum Wandern. _____
15. Du hältst die Landkarte falsch herum. _____
16. Er ist krank vor Angst. _____
17. Ihre Augen waren vor Entsetzen weit (aufgerissen). _____

## 3 Vocabulary: Find the missing words

let off steam • Frenchman • homeless • lovesick • useless • get off • seasick • hopeless • Dutchman • fall off • homesick • Englishman

1. Romeo and Juliet were _____ .
2. On a boat in strong wind you may get _____ .
3. Far away from friends and family you might get _____ .
4. When you are very angry, you might want to _____ .
5. Without a helmet you might get hurt when you _____ your bike.
6. You can _____ the bus at any stop you like.
7. A _____ usually likes wine and cheese.
8. A true _____ will probably drink his tea with milk.
9. A _____ is someone who comes from the Netherlands.
10. People who have no place to live are _____ .
11. If you have nothing to look forward to, your situation is rather _____ .
12. Something that is good for nothing is _____ .

## 4 Writing: Paraphrasing

Explain what the **marked** expressions mean by paraphrasing them.

1. Many people watched the fight, but nobody wanted to get **involved**.
2. It really was a big **feast** when John and Diana got married.
3. He **enclosed** a 20 dollar bill in his letter.
4. They couldn't **provide** us with **appropriate** shoes before we started our mountain tour.
5. Do you have any **coins** on you? I'd like to buy a newspaper.
6. Did you hear that my younger brother has got **engaged** to a girl from his college?
7. They **obviously** made a mistake when they packed the keyboard for my computer.

## 5 Vocabulary: Crossword puzzle

**Down ↓**
1. Chairs, tables, cupboards, etc.
2. Something that is easy to see or to understand is …
3. Wood that is used for building.
4. To give someone the idea for something (e.g. a poem, a song).
5. A plan that you make for the future, usually with somebody else.
8. Noun of 'angry'.

**Across →**
6. The person who tells a story.
7. The world or area we live in; everything around us.
9. Another word for 'police officer'.
10. A line of people who are waiting, e.g. at a bus stop or at the supermarket.
11. You type on it when you use your computer.

# unit 4

## 6 Listening: An interesting job

**7** Listen to track 7 and put the parts of the story about Mr Fox's watch in the right order.

1. Mr Fox tells the pupils to write an essay.
2. Mr Fox puts the book on the table.
3. A girl draws a cartoon of Mr Fox on the board.
4. Mr Fox looks surprised.
5. Mr Fox asks the pupils if they have seen the watch.
6. Mr Fox leaves the classroom.
7. [1] Mr Fox enters the classroom looking worried.
8. Mr Fox lifts the book up and finds the watch.
9. Mr Fox comes back into the classroom carrying a book.
10. Mr Fox says his watch has been stolen.

## 7 Listening: A short history of the *Mayflower*

**8 a)** Before listening to track 8 make sure you know what these two words mean. Then listen to the text.

> **voyage:** a journey often by sea
> **anniversary:** a day on which something special or historical is remembered; it's a bit like a birthday

**b)** Decide if these 20 statements are true, false or not in the text. Listen again and check your answers.

| | true | false | not in the text |
|---|---|---|---|
| 1. In 1620, a ship called the **Mayflower** sailed to America. | ✓ | | |
| 2. The **Mayflower** was very big. | | | |
| 3. The **Speedwell** was painted blue and white. | | | |
| 4. The **Mayflower** was 11 years old in 1620. | | | |
| 5. John Carver was French. | | | |
| 6. Only men travelled to America. | | | |
| 7. The **Mayflower** sailed from Southampton on August 15th. | | | |
| 8. They turned back twice because too much water was coming into the **Mayflower**. | | | |
| 9. The **Speedwell** was carrying 102 passengers. | | | |
| 10. The voyage took 65 days. | | | |
| 11. The **Mayflower** arrived in America on November 5th. | | | |
| 12. 41 men agreed on the **Mayflower** Compact. | | | |
| 13. John Carver was not the first leader. | | | |
| 14. Plymouth in America was named after Plymouth in England. | | | |
| 15. The **Mayflower's** passengers did not have enough food on the ship. | | | |
| 16. The winter of 1620–1621 was terrible. | | | |
| 17. The **Mayflower** arrived back in England on June 16th. | | | |
| 18. In 1957, a ship called the **Mayflower II** was built by America as a present to England. | | | |
| 19. The **Mayflower II** had no engine. | | | |
| 20. The **Mayflower II** is now in Plymouth, Massachusetts. | | | |

# New England

let's check

## 1 Grammar: Gerunds and infinitives

Fill in the correct verb forms, add prepositions and make other necessary changes.

1. Some boys in our class _____ (crazy • smoke) until our    /3

   teacher showed us photos of _____ (smoke) can do to your lungs.    /2

2. _____ (you • look    /3

   forward • invite) all your friends to the party on Saturday?

3. Are you keen _____ (swim)? Or would    /2

   _____ (you • prefer • go) for a walk along the beach?    /1

4. Mr and Mrs Smith _____    /3

   (dream • have) their own house ever since they got married. In the end they

   _____ (decide • build) one themselves.    /2

5. My girlfriend _____ (want • be) a singer in our rock band,    /2

   but I think she is _____ (real • bad • sing).    /3

6. When I was still at university, I couldn't _____ (imagine • do) a    /1

   regular job, which also _____ (mean • get up) early.    /2

7. "What _____ (spend) a few days at the seaside in a nice little    /2

   fishing port? Would you _____ (interested • do) that?    /2

8. In a big city like Boston, Mike _____    /4

   (simple • cannot • get used • live) in an apartment all by himself.

9. We suggested _____ (go • hike) in the mountains, but Susan    /2

   was so worried _____ (drive) on icy roads that we    /2

   _____ (decide • not • do) it in the end.    /2

10. Bill never complained _____ (have • work)    /2

    long hours. And he _____ (not •    /3

    worry • be paid) enough because he simply liked _____ (do) his job. He never    /1

    _____ (expect • be fired) without warning.    /2

11. My uncle prefers _____ (drive) to _____ (be driven).    /2

    But he can't stand _____ (sit) behind the steering wheel for too long.    /1

12. _____ (want • me • check) the solutions for you now?    /2

Now check your solutions and see how many points you've got:    /50

## 2 Mediation: Role player at the Pilgrim Village

Say it in English by using infinitive constructions.

1. Ich möchte, dass die Leute erkennen, dass das Leben im 17. Jahrhundert nicht so einfach war.
2. Es war fast unmöglich für die Siedler, den ersten Winter zu überleben.
3. Die Pilgerväter waren nicht die Einzigen, die nach Amerika auswanderten.
4. Und sie waren nicht die Letzten, die aus religiösen Gründen über den Atlantik hierher kamen.

_____
_____
_____
_____
_____
_____
_____
_____

## 3 Grammar: Moving to Baltimore

Fill in the correct verb form.

**1.** stay · follow · know · must move · be

I _____ Tom Taylor _____ (seit) more than five years now. Unfortunately his father _____ to Baltimore two months ago. Tom and his mother _____ _____ him next spring. If Tom _____ here in Boston, I _____ much happier.

**2.** not worry · feel · sit · like · give · tell

Look, there's Tom's grandmother. She _____ by the window all afternoon. – I wonder how she _____ it when she's taken to the old people's home next month. Only yesterday Tom said he _____ sorry he _____ her so much trouble recently, but his mother _____ him _____ so much.

**3.** hear · go · be · sleep · talk · not hear

A few days ago his grandmother _____ in her armchair when Tom and I _____ into the room, so she _____ what we _____ about. If she _____ awake, she _____ how much Tom worries about her.

**4.** spend · finish · celebrate · build

The Taylors' new house _____ at the moment, and Mr Taylor hopes it _____ _____ by the end of next month, so that they can _____ their Christmas holidays together. They _____ New Year's Eve with their friends.

# revision 2 — Units 3+4

## 1 Grammar: Travelling is fun!?

Fill in the correct verb form, add 'since' or 'for' and missing prepositions.

Mr and Mrs Barnett _____ (know) each other _____ more than 30 years. They both like _____ (get to know) other countries. They _____ (make) trips to almost every country in Europe _____ they _____ (meet) for the first time _____ college. Mr Barnett _____ (be) a businessman _____ he _____ (finish) college in 1983. He likes _____ (fly) a lot and he _____ (fly) to the USA _____ business regularly.

Last month, the Barnetts _____ (travel) _____ Paris together. Before that, they _____ (learn) French _____ at least six months. And they _____ (teach) a lot of useful expressions by Monsieur Dubois, their French neighbour. Mrs Barnett enjoys _____ (travel) with her husband. Sometimes she wonders if they _____ (ever • go) to Turkey together, because she'd like to see Istanbul so much. But today it's Rome. They _____ (wait) for their flight _____ eight in the morning and they _____ (just • tell) by an airline official that their plane _____ (still • service)¹. _____ (travel) abroad is not always fun after all!

¹[sɜːvɪs] – warten, technisch überprüfen

## 2 Mixed bag: Error-spotting

Underline the mistake and write the correct word on the right. There is one mistake in each sentence.

1. It's top secret, but she'll tell you when you promise not to inform her boss. _____
2. If Harry would have a new car, he would show it to everybody, I'm sure. _____
3. If Christopher doesn't arrive soon, we start watching the DVD without him. _____
4. If you will fly to Chicago with Lufthansa before 15th of June, it will cost you only 350 euros. _____
5. You can't enter this building when you do not show your identity card. _____
6. If I had known that there was plenty of time, I hadn't taken a taxi to get here. _____
7. Margret wouldn't have asked you for help if she would have known how to do it herself. _____
8. My brother would tell you how to design your own homepage if he would know how to do it. _____
9. If you arrive in London, I'll meet you at Heathrow Airport. Don't worry, I won't be late. _____

fifty-one 51

# Unit 5 intro — Fame and fortune

## 1 Vocabulary: Crossword puzzle

1. Only.
2. He really likes being a teacher, teaching is his …
3. Flats in London are very expensive. They cost a …
4. Noun of 'famous'.
5. If you … something, you think it is really good.
6. Pupils who have a positive … to school, usually get better marks.
7. The negative side of something, e.g. a job.
8. If you … yourself to something, you spend a lot of time on it.
9. If you cannot imagine something happening, it's … your wildest dreams.
10. Real.
11. To try hard.

## 2 Grammar: Pop stars

Complete the sentences in a) with suitable words. Then rewrite the sentences to say what would be / might be / would have been, if things were / had been different.

1. a) Will Smith is so _____ because he works hard.

   b) If he _____

2. a) Avril Lavigne was in the right place at the right time when she was _____ .

   b) If she _____

3. a) Orlando Bloom enjoys _____ an actor very much because he likes _____ up and becoming somebody else.

   b) If he _____

4. a) Robbie Williams _____ his former band *Take That* in 1997, so today he is one of the world's top solo musicians.

   b) If Robbie _____

# The audition

language A — unit 5

## 1 Grammar: Adverbs

Choose one of the following adverbs and complete the sentences. Use each adverb only once.

usually   actually   unfortunately   generally   apparently   in fact   frankly   obviously   hopefully

1. The audience did not clap their hands – they _____ hadn't liked Mike's performance!
2. _____ Mike had a cold, so his voice sounded strange.
3. _____ , his performance was a disaster!
4. _____ the next singer will be better!
5. _____ the audiences at shows like "Pop Idol"[1] go crazy.
6. _____ they actually throw things onto the stage.
7. _____ that happens quite often.
8. But _____ they behave well.
9. _____ the next boy, who has just started singing, is better – great!

[1]British version of *Deutschland sucht den Superstar*

## 2 Cloze test: The contest[1]

Complete the text.

Many of the young people who _____ part in contests like "Pop Idol" _____ never been heard of again. Although _____ of people watched them on TV, _____ anybody remembers their names today. Even _____ they had one or two hit _____ in the charts, they did not _____ a fortune with them, as _____ young people like to think. Once they _____ spent all their money, most of _____ went back to what they had _____ doing before they became famous for a couple of weeks. Others tried hard _____ stay in the spotlight[2] for a _____ longer – even if it was by _____ scandals or moving into a container _____ a while in order to be _____ 24 hours a day. But even _____ of their former fans who had _____ them most were soon no longer _____ in them. Some got the chance _____ record a complete album, but only _____ few of them have really become _____ artists. Some others got into trouble _____ the police, and a few even _____ to kill themselves – or actually did!

[1]['kɒntest] – Wettbewerb • [2]['spɒtlaɪt] – Rampenlicht

fifty-three 53

## 3 Writing: The pool

Make sentences. Think about the word order and the verb forms.

1. pool • Clyde • summer • often • the • to • go • in

_____

2. not like • much • obviously • very • swimming • he • but

_____

3. never • the • we • water • in fact • see • in • him • actually

_____

4. not be • swim • particularly • on • I • keen • actually

_____

5. I • hot • usually • days • into • really • on • jump • pool • the • for a minute • but

_____

6. Clyde • be • apparently • water • or • afraid • swim • not can • of • perhaps • but • he

_____

## 4 Mediation / Writing: Meet your favourite pop star!

Imagine you have won tickets for a concert by your favourite pop star. After the concert you will even have the chance to talk to him. He doesn't speak German, so you have to think of questions you would like to ask him in English. Write down the questions you and your friends have collected.

Wir wollen wissen, …
1. … wie er es geschafft hat, so erfolgreich zu sein.
2. … ob er oft zum Vorsingen mit anderen jugendlichen Teilnehmern (= *Künstlern*) gehen musste.
3. … ob seine Eltern ihn dazu ermutigten, Popstar zu werden.
4. … ob er ein sehr ehrgeiziger Mensch ist.
5. … ob es ihm nichts ausmacht, so viel Zeit in Hotels zu verbringen.
6. … ob er sich bei einem seiner Konzerte jemals in ein Mädchen aus dem Publikum verliebt hat.

_____

_____

_____

_____

_____

_____

_____

# After the audition

language B unit 5

## 1 Speaking: Formal and informal English

a) Decide which sentences are formal and which are informal English.
b) Underline the words or phrases that tell you and give a short explanation on the right. The words and phrases in the tip on the right may help you.
c) Find the pairs that belong together and number them like this: f1, f2 etc. (= formal) i1, i2 etc. (= informal).

**tip**
**formal:** subclauses, passive voice, exact, long forms, words of Latin / French origin, formal vocabulary;
**informal:** simple sentences, active voice; exaggeration; short forms simple / colloquial vocabulary

| | | |
|---|---|---|
| We were kept waiting for nearly 45 minutes. | f1 | passive voice, exact |
| I wish to apologize for being so rude to you. | | |
| As I was having a really interesting conversation with a young man I had met at the airport, I wasn't keen on boarding the plane. | | |
| They left us sitting there for hours. | i1 | exaggeration, colloquial |
| We spend considerable sums of money on eating out. | | |
| Her house is in the middle of nowhere. | | |
| She lives in a village that is located about 20 km away from the nearest town. | | |
| I had a chat with that guy out there. Didn't feel like hopping on the plane. | | |
| Sorry, I shouldn't have called you names. | | |
| We fork out tons of money on food and drink in pubs. | | |

## 2 Mixed bag: Error-spotting

Find the mistake in each line, underline the wrong word and write down the correct one on the right.

After the audition Mrs Simons told Mrs Denker at the phone what had _____

happened. She complained about the way in which the hole event had _____

been organised, and particular about the fact that they had been kept _____

waiting for a condiserable time before the director arrived. Another _____

thing she had not appreciated was the unnecessary large number of _____

hopeful young performers who had invited to the audition. When Mrs _____

Denker asked if Billy had received a backcall yet, that made her even _____

more angry, and she promised writing a letter. _____

fifty-five 55

# Unit 5 language B

## 3 Writing: A letter of complaint

**a)** Dave from London went on a coach trip to watch a football match in Hamburg. Read what he told his friend Alan on the phone after he had come back home.

Hi Alan, It's me, Dave!
I've just come back from Hamburg. (…) What it was like? It was hell! (…) Well, let me start with the drive to Hamburg. You know how long it took us to get to the ferry? Four hours! (…) Well, we had to pick up quite a few people, and some of them in the middle of nowhere, too! So we missed our ferry and had to wait for the next one – so no more sightseeing in Hamburg. The next shock came when I found out that I didn't have a single room. There was another man in my room! (…) Then I had to take the underground to the stadium, because the coach had disappeared. (…) Of course I got there more than half an hour late, but what was even worse was my seat! It was right behind one of the goals! (…) At night I could not sleep because of all the cars going past! (…) The breakfast in the morning was a joke – just coffee and toast! (…) And then all that way back home again! What a trip! (…) You can be sure of that, I'll write them a letter immediately! They have to give me some of my money back! See you tomorrow, Alan. Bye!

**b)** Complete Dave's formal letter of complaint to the coach company.

42 Queens Drive
London
5th March

The Football Coach
21 Upper Street
London

Dear _____ ,

I _____ to _____ about the coach trip _____ _____ on 3rd and 4th March. As a large _____ of people had to _____ c_____ from different towns and _____ on the way, we were not able to take the 12 o'clock ferry as p_____ . As a r_____ of this there was no c_____ for me to go _____ in Hamburg. In the hotel in Hamburg I was _____ _____ a single room, but had to _____ a room with a man who was _____ to me. As the coach was nowhere to _____ outside the hotel, I was _____ to take the underground to the stadium, so I _____ there half an hour after _____ had _____ . In spite of having _____ and _____ for a seat on the grandstand[1], my seat was behind one of the goals, which _____ that I was not _____ to see very well. At night it was nearly _____ for me to sleep, as the hotel was located in a very _____ street. Finally, the breakfast in the morning was of _____ q_____ , too. In _____ of all this, I _____ you to _____ part of the _____ I paid for the whole package and look _____ to _____ from you very soon.

Yours _____ , David Finch

[1] ['grændstænd] – Haupttribüne

## 4 Reading: American Idol

Complete the text – as shown in line 1 – with the words in the box.

> decide • young • laugh • people • in front of • audition • can't • ~~popular~~ • first • become • usually • call • best • their

"American Idol" is a very **popular** programme on American TV, and especially _____ people love it. It is a talent contest[1] in which TV viewers can _____ in and vote[2] for the _____ performers to discover the singer with the most talent. In the _____ round of the contest thousands of _____ teenagers _____ in cities all over the US. They have to sing _____ a jury of three people who must _____ which of the hopeful young artists will make it to the second round. The jury members are quite strict[3], but sometimes they choose performers who _____ sing at all, because that makes it funnier for the _____ who watch the show on TV! Some people have _____ famous because _____ performances were so bad that they made millions of TV viewers _____ at them!

[1] ['kɒntest] – Wettbewerb • [2] [vəʊt] – (ab)stimmen, wählen • [3] [strɪkt] – streng

## 5 Mixed bag: The song contest[1]

Matt is talking to his friend about Marty McKenna, one of their classmates. Fill in the verbs in the correct tense – simple or progressive, active or passive. Sometimes you have to add *to* or a preposition, and there are negative forms, too.

Matt: Gary, _____ you _____ (read) the news about Marty in today's newspaper? He _____ (sing) in a song contest next month.

Gary: No, I _____ (have) a chance to read today's newspaper yet. But I _____ (wait) Marty since half past two. This morning he _____ (say) me that he _____ (meet) his 'manager' Alex at two o'clock. After that, he _____ (want) come here, but so far he _____ (arrive).

Matt: That's strange, because I _____ (try • call) him half an hour ago, but he _____ (already • leave) his parents' house then. At least that's what I _____ (tell) by his mum. But Mrs McKenna _____ (be) very busy. She _____ (make) dinner when I rang (ring).

Gary: Well, if Marty _____ (be) here by six o'clock, I _____ (call) Alex, although I don't _____ (like) him very much.

[1] ['kɒntest] – Wettbewerb

## 6 Mixed bag: British or American English?

Read the following extract from Linda's diary. She lives in a big city – but in which country? Underline the 27 words or phrases that tell you if she is British or American. Write down the "other" words, phrases or ways of spelling on the extra lines.

Dear diary,                                                                 Thursday, 12 Jan 2006

<u>I've just come</u> back from a great theatre and dance performance at school. It started at
<u>I just came</u>

quarter past six and lasted until nine o'clock, but it was never boring. The dancers must have
___

been practising for months, and our headteacher said that most of them had not even been on
___

holiday since autumn. They were wearing special trousers with both legs a different colour.
___

That made a lot of the younger pupils laugh, but it is not the sort of humour I like. But the play
___

itself was great! My neighbour Sue was there, too. I'd gone by underground, but we took
___

a taxi home which Sue had called on her mobile. While we were waiting for it, we shared
___

a bag of chips. At the weekend, Sue's parents are going to London to watch a football match,
___

so we can use their flat for a party! Sue said we could watch our favourite programmes on TV
___

and told me to bring some crisps. We haven't got any crisps at home, but I think
___

sweets will be OK, too, and I've already taken some out of the cupboard in the kitchen.
___

I'm really tired now, so I'll go to sleep.

# A song project

## 1 Speaking: Adverbs

Look at the following statements. Add one adverb of degree and one adverb of comment to each of them. Don't use any adverb more than once!

> utterly   of course   at all   appartently
> completely   even   actually   really
> absolutely   frankly   in fact   fortunately

1. You're an ignorant person!

   _____ , you're a _____ ignorant person!

2. You're bored by what I'm saying, aren't you?

   _____ you're _____ bored by what I'm saying, aren't you?

3. I think you don't know the singer I'm talking about!

   _____ I think you don't _____ know the singer I'm talking about.

4. You've no idea about music!

   _____ you've no idea about music _____ !

5. I know you think I should change my style of music.

   _____ I know you think I should change my style of music _____ .

6. But I don't need your useless advice!

   But _____ I don't need your _____ useless advice!

## 2 C-test: The talent show

Complete the missing words.

Last year there was an audition in my hometown for one of the big t_____ shows on German TV. A friend of m_____ , who thinks he is a r_____ good rapper, wanted to t_____ part in it, and of c_____ we all e_____ him to go. He is quite a_____ , and when he has a d_____ , he works h_____ for it to come true. On the day of the audition, he s_____ up at the gym where it was taking p_____ in his wildest hip hop clothes. He said they w_____ give him c_____ on the stage, so that he wouldn't be too n_____ . Well, it is not an e_____ to say that he was u_____ shocked when he was t_____ that he would have to sing to piano a_____ ! In fact he wanted to c_____ the whole thing, and it r_____ a lot of encouragement from us to p_____ him from doing so! When it w_____ his turn, his p_____ was better t_____ ever – it s_____ like hip hop with a bit of Mozart! I'm c_____ that he will r_____ a callback.

## 3 Listening: Stage school audition

**a)** Before you listen to track 9, look at this information:

> **Don't beat about the bush:** If somebody is taking too much time or too many words to say something.
> **Get a move on:** Hurry up!

**b)** Now listen and tick (✔) the correct answer for each question. Be careful! The questions are not in the order you listened to them!

**c)** Listen again to check your answers.

1. Why doesn't Mike's dad go to school theatre performances?
   a) He doesn't like Shakespeare.
   b) He has to watch TV.
   c) He has no time.

2. What does Mike's mother think about Mike's plans?
   a) She's unhappy.
   b) She's scared.
   c) She's pleased.

3. At the audition Mike had to act some scenes. How many?
   a) Two.
   b) Three.
   c) Four.

4. What did Mike *not* have to do at the audition?
   a) He did not have to sing.
   b) He did not have to dance.
   c) He did not have to act.

5. Which college does Mike's dad want him to go to?
   a) The farming college.
   b) The business college.
   c) The teaching college.

6. Which museum did the boys go to?
   a) The British Museum.
   b) The Science Museum.
   c) The History Museum.

7. Where is Mike's stage school?
   a) It's in Birmingham.
   b) It's in London.
   c) It's in Liverpool.

8. What is Mike's dad's job?
   a) He's a teacher.
   b) He's a farmer.
   c) He's a vet.

## 4 Listening: A rock star

**a)** Listen carefully to track 10 and answer the following questions. **b)** Listen again to check your answers.

1. What is the name of Jazzie's rock band and who thought of it first?

2. How many musicians are there in the band. What are their names?

3. What do most people think about rock stars?

4. Why did Basher stop talking?

5. What is one of the hardest things about being a rock star?

6. What is bad about being on tour?

7. What does the rock band do between tours?

# Fame and fortune

**let's check** unit 5

## 1 Grammar: Adverbs
Write the sentences again with the adverbs in the best positions.

1. Directors are not nice to teenage performers. (**generally • really**)

   _____

2. So Tina was worried, although she had no reason to be. (**absolutely • a bit**)

   _____

3. The singer who sang before her did not do well. (**particularly • fortunately**)

   _____

4. But Tina did not need any help, her performance was great! (**simply • actually**)

   _____

## 2 Vocabulary: Word power
Complete the grid.

| Noun | Verb | Adjective | Adverb |
|---|---|---|---|
| appearance | | | apparently |
| completion | | | |
| | – | fortunate | |
| | | | hopefully |
| | – | lucky | |
| surprise | | a)<br>b) | |

## 3 Writing: Weekend activities
Put the words in the right order.

1. Marcus • sleeps • at the weekend • often • until 10 o'clock

   _____

2. Tina • goes • on Saturdays • usually • to the youth club

   _____

3. Paul • visits • sometimes • on Sunday • his grandparents • in Leeds

   _____

4. Clara • has • unfortunately • to work • once a month • at her aunt's hotel.

   _____

sixty-one **61**

# 3 focus
## Focus on international contacts

### 1 Mediation: Off to Australia on a Working Holiday Visa!

Lies die folgenden Informationen zu der Möglichkeit, Australien mit einem *Working Holiday Visa* zu erkunden. Schlage alle unbekannten Wörter nach, die du brauchst, um die wichtigen Details zu verstehen und beantworte dann die Fragen – auf Deutsch, aber mit Erklärungen!

**Working Holiday Makers**

The Working Holiday Program provides opportunities for people between 18 and 30 to holiday in Australia and to supplement their travel funds through incidental employment. Australia has reciprocal Working Holiday Maker arrangements in effect with the United Kingdom, Canada, the Netherlands, Japan, Republic of Ireland, Republic of Korea, Malta, Germany, Denmark, Sweden, Norway, the Hong Kong Special Administrative Region (HKSAR) of the People's Republic of China, Finland, the Republic of Cyprus, France, Italy, Belgium, Estonia and Taiwan. The visa allows a stay of up to 12 months from the date of first entry into Australia, regardless of whether or not you spend the whole time in Australia. You are allowed to do any kind of work of a temporary or casual nature, and you can work with each employer for up to three months. Working Holiday Makers who have worked as a seasonal worker in Regional Australia for a minimum of three months while on their first Working Holiday visa, will be eligible to apply for a second Working Holiday visa. Applicants need to demonstrate that they continue to meet the requirements for a Working Holiday visa. These include:
– being aged between 18 and 30
– having no dependents; and
– being a citizen of a country named in the Working Holiday Maker reciprocal arrangements. **Seasonal work** is defined as: picking fruit, nuts and other crops, […] and other work associated with packing or processing the harvest. **Regional Australia** includes anywhere in Australia except Sydney, Newcastle, Wollongong, the New South Wales Central Coast, Brisbane, the Gold Coast, Perth, Melbourne or the Australian Capital Territory. If you intend to apply for a second Working Holiday visa, you will need to provide evidence that you have worked for a minimum of three months as a seasonal worker in regional Australia while on your first Working Holiday visa. […] Acceptable evidence of seasonal work for Working Holiday Makers who undertook seasonal work in regional Australia may be original or certified copies of payslips … and other employer references. There are two ways to apply for the Working Holiday visa. They are:
– on the Internet
– by mail; you can download an application form from the official website of the Department of Immigration and Multicultural Affairs: www.immi.gov.au

1. Bekomme ich als Deutscher ein *Working Holiday Visa* (WHV)? _____

2. Wie kann ich ein *WHV* beantragen? _____

3. Wie lange ist ein *WHV* gültig? _____

4. Verlängert sich die Gültigkeitsdauer, wenn ich dazwischen drei Monate nach Neuseeland fliege?
_____

5. Mein Onkel ist 32 und möchte ein *WHV* beantragen. Geht das? _____

6. Kann ich ein halbes Jahr für einen Arbeitgeber arbeiten? _____

7. Wer kann nach Ablauf des ersten ein zweites *WHV* beantragen? _____

8. Kann man mit kleinen Kindern ein *WHV* beantragen? _____

# Up to Unit 5 — revision 3

## 1 Grammar: What if …?

Read the following sentences about animals in Australia. Rewrite them to say what would be / might be / would have been if things were / had been different.

1. Kangaroos have strong tails which help them to jump high in the air.

   _____

   _____

2. Koalas needn't drink water because they eat enough leaves.

   _____

   _____

3. Wombats sleep during the day, so they are hardly ever spotted by tourists.

   _____

   _____

4. Emus have always been hunted by the Aborigines because their meat tastes so good.

   _____

   _____

5. The Tasmanian tiger was hunted to extinction[1] because it ate the farmers' sheep.

   _____

   _____

[1] [ɪkˈstɪŋkʃn] – Ausrottung

## 2 Grammar: Active or passive?

Fill in the verbs in the correct tense – active or passive, simple or progressive. Add *by* where necessary.

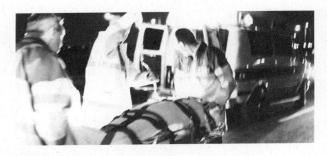

Last night Jack _____ (wake up) a loud noise in front of his bedroom window. When he _____ (look) out, he _____ (see) that an accident _____ (happen). When he _____ (open) the window, he _____ (ask) a man if he had a telephone. Jack said, "Yes, of course", but a second later he _____ (remember) that he _____ (drop) his phone on the floor the day before and it _____ (not repair) yet. Suddenly the sound of an ambulance _____ (could hear) – apparently it _____ (call) the other driver. But in the end it _____ (not need) because nobody _____ (injure • seriously) in the accident.

sixty-three **63**

## revision 3

### 3 Grammar: Gerund or infinitive?

Complete the following story told by sixteen-year-old Carolyn, who moved from Melbourne to Cairns near the Great Barrier Reef after her mother had been offered a good job up there. Fill in the gerund or the infinitive with *to*. Add prepositions where necessary.

After Mum and I had decided _____ (leave) Melbourne, we got really excited about _____ (go) up to Cairns _____ (look) for a nice flat. Before we left, my mum told me _____ (not forget) to say goodbye to my grandparents, and I suggested _____ (have) breakfast with them before we left. In fact, I was a little worried about _____ (leave) the two old people behind in Melbourne. But then the last words my grandma said to me before we left were, "And you know I don't want you _____ (wear) those mini-skirts," so that made things a little easier for me! How often she managed _____ (drive) me crazy with sentences like that! Our trip to Cairns was great, and it was hard _____ (say) what was more fascinating: the ocean or the look on Mum's face. _____ (be) together with her that day was great. She preferred _____ (drive) all night _____ (stay) in a hotel, so we only stopped _____ (get) gas and _____ (take) pictures. After we had crossed the border into Queensland, she hardly stopped _____ (drive) at all, and I didn't mind _____ (listen) to all her stories. And suddenly I was not afraid of _____ (leave) my friends in Melbourne any more, but was already looking forward to _____ (make) new ones in Cairns.